PURGATORY: Divine Mercy

PURGATORY
Divine Mercy

PILGRIMS OF LOVE FOUNDATION
PLF

MARINO RESTREPO

First edition published in Mexico by P.L.F.
September, 2013 – 5,000 copies

Diagram and Design: Maria Heneghan
Cover Design: Luz Angela Garcia Betancur
Cover Photograph: Pilgrims of Love Mission
Randalstown, Northern Ireland

Original Spanish edition
Translated by: Virginia Marie Forrester
Biblical texts taken from the Navarre Bible.
EUNSA Popular Edition.

Send requests to: PILGRIMS OF LOVE FOUNDATION
pilgrimsofloveuk.ireland@gmail.com
Visit our Website: www.marinorestrepo.com
Pilgrims of love
P.O.Box 830
Wembley, HA9 1AQ

This book is written to enrich the knowledge of Catholics about the wonderful gift of the mercy of God for souls. Who, on dying and appearing before the Divine Tribunal of our Lord Jesus Christ, without a perfect and holy preparation, are rescued from the punishment of eternal damnation and taken to live in a state of purification or purgation. Where, after passing through a trial by fire, they have the opportunity to enter into the fullness of the eternal glory of Paradise.

The first part of the book is a compilation of excerpts from the Councils, in which the existence of Purgatory is established as a dogmatic reality for the Catholic believer. The second part is a collection of testimonies of mystics and saints of the Church, who have left a valuable legacy of information on their experiences with souls in Purgatory and of their innumerable sufferings. They are useful to us as profound reflections on the responsibilities we all have in our preparation for the days we face after our death. The third part is a testimony of the author's mystical experience, which enables one to share the depth of his vision of the sufferings souls endure in Purgatory.

The essential message of this book is to present the infinite Mercy of God, which continues even after our death.

CONTENTS

FOREWORD

At the present time there are many difficulties affecting the life of the Church; however this book will focus only on the examination of one of the truths detailed in the Catechism of the Church: Purgatory. It is true that, in the post-conciliar years, the ecclesial Magisterium has had to intervene in certain circumstances, with its infallible authority, to defend the truth of the Deposit of the Faith, which is conveyed by Sacred Scripture and Sacred Tradition. Indeed such intervention is needed, now even more ardently in this new millennium, the church should follow the mandate that our Lord Jesus Christ gave to Peter, when He told him, that he must confirm the faith of all his brethren (cf. *Luke* 22:31-32).

Sadly, many Christians who call themselves Catholics, seem unable to understand the important need to adhere to, and unite with the teachings of the Magisterium. By recognising the catechesis of the Church they can avoid the danger of being drawn 'by the winds of doctrines' and taught moral and doctrinal errors which are promoted by many anti-ecclesial environments, national governments and religious sects.

Never has man been in greater need of a sure norm of life, which will enable him to have a clear understanding of moral and ethical values. It is precisely because of such an erosion of ethical behavior, that we are also facing an astounding loss of the basic foundations of the faith. To the extent that, within the Catholic Church herself, we are seeing total disorder and confusion in relation to the main object of the act of faith: what should be believed, and who should be believed.

In such a situation, it is easy to find 'Catholics' who have let themselves be swayed, and guided, by new doctrines that gratify their conscience, allowing them to live as they please. Subjective conscience has become the accepted behavior and the infallible teaching of the Magisterium is accepted, only in so far as it conforms to their way of thinking. If not, it is simply not accepted.

This book, which touches upon one of the truths of our faith – that today is widely doubted – is the fruit of the wide ecclesial experience of the author. The experience of a great sinner who converted and, more than that, was rescued after many years of estrangement from the Church. He was rescued as the result of a true mystical experience, in which our Lord Jesus Christ manifested His infinite Mercy to him.

In his first book, entitled *Testimony,* the author describes the astonishing and most extraordinary experience of his conversion. After that event, and for the past 15 years, Marino Restrepo has traveled around the world, visiting more than 105 countries. He has preached tirelessly; guided by his personal experience, he presents the true faith in keeping with the orthodox teaching of the Church, and the content of the Deposit of the Faith.

While defending the truth, he unmasks the lies and errors of false doctrines, which dull the minds and consciences of many weak Catholics, who lack clear and sufficient knowledge of the Church's teachings. These false doctrines have caused many Catholics to be shaken like reeds in the wind, and so, have risked apostatising from the true faith.

It is a thorough book, well documented with biblical and magisterial teachings, and enriched by the experiences of Saints and mystics, who were exposed to the reality of Purgatory. To the testimony of these Saints, the author adds his own experience, exactly as he lived it. This includes a reflection upon the sin of adultery in his own life.

We never fully consider the consequences of our acts on others. The text makes it clear, that in Purgatory we will have to meticulously purify for all the negative consequences that our sins have had on the lives of others, especially if it caused them to sin.

The book provides clarification on the graces of Indulgences; graces that the Mother Church grants for the spiritual wellbeing of her children, in order to help them to do reparation for their faults, whilst remaining in this world, with the hope of diminishing their purification after death. Very appropriate, therefore, is the lovely prayer book of supplications for the dead, with which the author ends the book. It reviews the ways to gain plenary and partial indulgences as established by the Church.

This document will certainly be of great help to Catholics who need to be more aware of the realities and duties of their Christian life in relation to the hereafter. This is well expressed in the phrase 'the Communion of Saints,' and proclaimed in the Apostles' Creed. The book seeks not only to dispel doubts about the existence of Purgatory, but also to awaken and revive in the reader, charity towards suffering souls, who are most in need of our prayers and intercessions.

In the name of the whole Church, I wish to thank the author of this book, for this new testimony of life and service to Her. His written work is no less effective than the word he preaches around the world.

Finally it is to Jesus and his Most Holy Mother that we address our gratitude, for all the wonderful work they have done and will do with this chosen instrument, for the good of many more brethren.

For the glory of God and of His Church.

Friar Joseph Mary of the Five Wounds F.M.R
Spiritual Father of Marino Restrepo

PRESENTATION

I believe in the Communion of Saints, the forgiveness of sins, the resurrection of the body and life everlasting.

We repeat this formula often. It forms part of the profession of faith that we have received, which guides us as we walk on this earth and opens us up to *eternal blessedness.* It is faith, a gift of God, which opens up to us, the way of hope and leads us to the *eternal life* of which, *the Lord,* the Son of God, the Son of Man speaks to us; He for whom everything was created, the first-born of humanity.

Living the joy of our faith, we walk without pausing, desirous of attaining the fullness of life. And while we walk, we must nourish ourselves to continue walking and to quicken our step, in order to enter the divine nuptial banquet to which we have been invited.

We nourish ourselves with the *Word.* We nourish ourselves with fraternal celebration in the faith; with the *living bread,* with the joy of intimacy; when we experience the closeness of the affection of our *Father,* who loves us and awaits us; when we know and feel that He forgives us; when He receives us despite our limitations and sins. It is in humble and confident prayer, whilst in dialogue with the One who loves us, that we are nourished and have the certainty that His merciful love purifies, cleanses, and clothes us with a radiant garment to enter into the fullness of endless joy.

We are also nourished by putting our precious gift of reason to work. This gives us arguments, reflection and the growing dynamism of spiritual, mental, psychic, emotional and corporal progress; all of which spells personal growth in the plan that God has for us, His children, in the permanent seeking of love, of the perfect, of the holy, with the vehement desire to be like HIM, to be 'Saints'.

Precisely in this period of growth, of seeking, of dialogue, and of experiences, we receive Marino Restrepo's work, based on the wonderful patrimony of the Church, Mother and Teacher, who accompanies us on our pilgrimage. Here she encourages and protects us, on our path to reach the fullness of truth. In this period and for our nourishment and rational-spiritual growth, we receive the offer of *Purgatory*, of the state of certain hope for those who are at the door of the celebration of the 'Wedding Banquet'. A state of preparation that ensures the prize: *Eternal Life, Joyful Blessedness, Eternal Salvation*.

Purgatory is a state that duly prepares us for the enjoyment of praise forever, in perfect union with God, with HIM, who is for each one: 'My God', 'My Love', 'My All.' The Beloved who does not fail, who forgives me, who purifies me because He loves me and because He wants me to shine with His own light, as a true son or daughter of His love.

We are referring to the work compiled on Purgatory of a brother who feels called to share his experience of faith and love with all his brethren. This work can be for all readers an instrument that nourishes their spirit while walking as pilgrims towards eternal life. It tells us what the Church has done for humanity; of the reality of the believers walking towards the fullness of love to which we are called: eternal union with *love* itself.

Our hope is that on receiving this nourishment with humility, we thank God the Father and love our Mother 'The Church' evermore. In her wisdom, she has kept for us, in the course of the years, the message of truth which we now relish in this simple work compiled of sure doctrine, taken from the source of truth: the living tradition of the Church, faithful to God and to man.

This message should be read with humility, love and a spirit of prayer. Thus it will serve as a very good preparation to grow in the love of God and the fulfillment of His divine law, which is love.

Thank you and a blessing for all.

+ Jose de Jesus Quintero Diaz
Child of God, Servant of the Children of God,
Apostolic Vicar, Bishop of Leticia (Amazonas)

INTRODUCTION

The Catholic Church teaches us that the existence of Purgatory is so real that she has decreed it Dogma. This means that to consider oneself a Catholic and to profess the faith in obedience to the Church, one must believe this Dogma, otherwise we apostatise from our Catholic faith. It is simply that strict. We can say with certainty that any person who professes the Catholic faith, but denies the existence of Purgatory, whether he be laity, or a religious, ceases to be a Catholic.

Today it is very common to find both priests and laymen who deny the existence of Purgatory with ease, and in some cases, even reject it from the pulpit. It is very important for us, as Catholics to understand the fundamental truths of our faith, otherwise the countless erroneous theologies propagated today, including those found within the Catholic Church, could rob us of the foundations of our religion.

This book does not pretend to give a theological teaching. It is, on the contrary, an opportunity to review the information, written in simple language by a laymen. Who, without formation in Theology or Religious Sciences, wishes to share his personal experience of Jesus Christ; the truths revealed to the Catholic Church, perfectly documented in the Deposit of the Faith and the catalogue of testimonies from the Saints, meticulously compiled in our Sacred History. It is a duty of every Catholic to constantly observe the endless proposals that the world makes to us through human science, modern ideologies and philosophies that appear to be attractive alternatives.

In 15 years of missionary life around the world, I have frequently met Catholics who do not know, or understand the foundations of their faith. Moreover I observed many dioceses lacking a strong catechesis centered on building communities, which focus on the Sacred Tradition and Holy Doctrine of the Church. As a result, there is a huge amount of ignorance about what we must profess as Catholics, and what we are called to preach and defend with our lives.

Understanding the reality of Purgatory is vital for our spiritual growth. If we take an individual who has no knowledge of his ancestry – a person who is unaware of his father's identity, and compare him with someone who knows, and has a relationship with his father; he, by comparison, lacks the many necessary tools to strengthen his emotional integrity, his interior equilibrium. This applies equally to a Catholic who is not well versed in Doctrine or who, although knowing it, does not believe the truths that have been revealed to him through it. He professes his faith as he wishes which, in other words, means that he is ignorant of his faith; he lacks basic knowledge of his religious roots, and therefore, he has little religious integrity to nourish him for his spiritual edification.

The above picture is very common among modern Catholics. My intention in writing this book, therefore, is to give the ordinary reader access to information that, although not new, seems to have been widely overlooked. The ignorance of the modern-day Catholic's faith, is not limited to Purgatory; he is also ignorant of the vast majority of truths revealed to the Church.

A Catholic student of the University of Notre Dame, Indiana, said to me: 'It seems to be fashionable to deny the existence of Purgatory'. She was very worried and asked me anxiously: 'What can we do? When I hear a priest or a nun or a monk speak in such a way, I would like the earth to swallow them, to prevent them from causing further harm, but I know that this is not the way to solve things. What should we do? What happened to them? Who made such fools of them?'

The first chapters of this book are dedicated to presenting the official documentation of the Church, which certifies the existence of Purgatory. You will find the Councils that declare it and the mystical experiences of many Saints, whom God allowed to witness Purgatory in a very profound way, so that they may testify are testimonies of its existence. These faithful testimonies are given for the glory of God and the edification of his Church.

"Purgatory, necessary purification for the encounter with God"

Saint John Paul II

RECOMMENDATION

I ask the ordinary reader not to become too concerned about the classical and ancient language found in the Canons and Councils of the Church, quoted here in the first chapter. In referring to them, my intention is that the reader should gain a deeper and fuller understanding of the documents which form the structure of the Catholic faith. It should also be used as a source of sanctioned and reliable arguments, established by the Church, under the Deposit of Faith. With such access to this doctrine, the reader will be able to make a fitting defense of the existence of Purgatory, in line with the teachings of the Church.

The reader will also find some biblical quotations repeated in the different testimonies of the Saints and the Canons of the Church. These quotations are kept to maintain the fidelity and originality of the said testimonies and documents.

Purgatory:
The word comes from the Latin *purgare:* to cleanse, to purify.

In keeping with Catholic doctrine, it is a state or condition of temporal punishment for those who, leaving this life in the grace of God, are not free from the consequences of sin and want to do reparation to be worthy of heavenly goods.

Over the centuries the Catholic Church, in the fullness of her wisdom as guardian of the Deposit of the Faith, has pronounced and reaffirmed the truth of the Gospel. Thus we are therefore able to see how the Catholic Doctrine of Purgatory has been established through time, professed in the holy councils of the Church and documented in the Catholic Catechism. Indeed we see that the Church has always stayed faithful to the words of Scared Scripture and followed the teachings of Our Lord Jesus Christ to His apostles closely.

CANON OF THE CHURCH

The doctrine of Purgatory was declared a Dogma at the Council of Florence. The Council of Lyon had already affirmed its existence and the Council of Trent confirmed this Dogma against the Reformers. As we shall presently see, many other Councils established Purgatory as a reality for many souls after death.

A. COUNCILS OF THE CHURCH

I. FIRST COUNCIL OF LYON. YEAR 1245

'Affirming the truth in the Gospel that if someone should blaspheme against the Holy Spirit, he will not be forgiven either in this life or in the future, by which is understood that some offenses will be forgiven in this age and others in the age to come (*Matthew* 12:32), and the Apostle also says that fire will test what sort of work each one has done; and if any man's work is burned up, he will suffer loss, though he himself will be saved but only through fire (1 *Corinthians* 3:13 and 15) and as it is said that the Greeks themselves believe and affirm truly and indubitably that the souls of those that die, having received a penance but not fulfilled it or that are without mortal sin, but with venial and slight sin, are purified after death and can be helped by the suffrages of the Church.

But, given that it says that the place of this purification has not been indicated to her by her doctors with a sure and proper name, we who in keeping with the traditions and authorities of the Holy Fathers call it Purgatory, want it hence-forth to be called by this name also among them.

Because sins are certainly purged with that transitory fire, not the criminal or capital ones, which were not forgiven before by penance, but the small and slight ones which even after death still weigh, even if they were forgiven in life. But if someone dies in mortal sin without penance, he is without a doubt perpetually tormented by the burning of eternal Hell. However, the souls of small children who die after Baptism and also of adults who die in charity and are not held back either by sin or any satisfaction for it, fly without delay to the everlasting homeland."[1]

II. SECOND COUNCIL OF LYON. YEAR 1274

'Yet, because of different errors that some have introduced out of ignorance and others out of malice, [the Council] says and preaches that those who after Baptism fall into sin, are not to be baptised again, but obtain the forgiveness of sins through true penance. And if truly repentant they die in charity before having satisfied with worthy fruits of penance for their commissions and omissions, their souls are purified after death, with purgatory and punishments, as explained to us by Friar John; and for relief of those punishments they benefit from the suffrages of the living faithful, that is, the sacrifices of Masses, prayers and alms and other forms of piety that, in keeping with the institutions of the Church, some faithful undertake in favor of others.

1   "Catholic.net – First Council of Lyon (France). Year 1245."
N.p., n.d. Web. 02 Apr. 2013.

However, those souls that, after receiving Holy Baptism, did not incur in any sin, and also those souls that after contracting it have been purged, while they remained in their bodies or after being denuded of them, are received immediately into Heaven.'[2]

III. BENEDICTUS DEUS, BULL OF POPE BENEDICT. YEAR 1336

It defines that the souls of the just that do not need to be purged, enjoy immediately the vision of God and it also defines that those also, that have something to purify, will enjoy God once they are purified after death.[3]

IV. COUNCIL OF FERRARA, FLORENCE. YEARS 1438-1442

'This Council is also known as the Council of Basle, Ferrara and Florence because it passed through all these cities. If true penitents left this world before having satisfied with worthy fruits of penance for what they committed or omitted, their souls are purged with purifying punishments after their death and to be alleviated from these punishments, they benefit from the suffrages of the living faithful, such as the sacrifice of the Mass, prayers and alms and other forms of piety that the faithful usually practice for other faithful, in keeping with the institutions of the Church.

---

2   *"Catholic.net – Second Council of Lyon. Year 1274."* N.p., n.d. Web.02 Apr.2013.

3   H.H. Benedict XVI. *"On the Beatific Vision of God."* Benedictus Deus. N.p., n.d. Web. 02 Apr. 2013.

And that the souls of those who after receiving Baptism, did not incur absolutely in any stain of sin, and also those that, after contracting a stain of sin, have purged it either while they were living in their bodies or after they came out of them, according to what was said above, are immediately received in Heaven and see clearly God himself, One and Triune, just as He is, some, however, with greater perfection than others, in keeping with the diversity of their merits.' [464].

V. FIFTH LATERAN COUNCIL. YEAR 1512

'And so that henceforth no one can allege ignorance of the Doctrine of the Roman Church about these indulgences and their efficacy, or excuse himself with the pretext of such ignorance or with feigned declaration help himself, but that they can be convinced of being culpable of notorious lying and punished with reason, we have decided to express through the present letters that the Roman Church, which the rest are obliged to follow as Mother, teaches:

"That the Roman Pontiff, Successor of Peter, holder of the keys and Vicar of Jesus Christ on earth, by the power of the keys, which open the Kingdom of Heaven, removing from the faithful of Christ the impediments of their entrance (namely, the offense and punishment due to present sins: The offense through the Sacrament of Penance and the temporal punishment, in keeping with due justice for present sins, through the indulgence of the Church), can for reasonable causes grant to Christ's faithful themselves – that, by uniting them in charity, are members of Christ, be it in this life, be it in Purgatory –, indulgences of the super abundance of the merits of Christ and of the Saints; and that (the Roman Pontiff) granting indulgence with apostolic authority, both for the living as well as the dead, has usually dispensed the treasure of the merits of Christ and of the Saints conferring the indulgence itself by way of absolution or transferring it by way of suffrage."

And, therefore, that all, both living and dead, who have truly gained all these indulgences, are freed from all temporal punishment due, in keeping with Divine Justice, for their present sins, as equivalent to the indulgence already gained."[4]

VI. COUNCIL OF TRENT. YEAR 1545

This Council confirmed the doctrine of Purgatory against the Reformers. It defined: 'the imperfection of man's justice, imperfection that comes from the obligation of atonement for a sin meriting temporal punishment after absolution, for which reparation must be done in this life or in the next.'

The Council decreed:

'The Catholic Church, having taught in the Councils and very recently in this Ecumenical Synod, instructed by the Holy Spirit through the Sacred Scriptures and by the ancient tradition of the Fathers, that there is Purgatory and that the souls retained there are helped by the prayers of the faithful, but above all by the sacrifice of the altar, worthy of being accepted: the Holy Synod orders the bishops to endeavor diligently

4   "*Catholic.net – Fifth Lateran Council. Years 1512-1517.*" N.p., n.d. Web. 02 Apr. 2013.

that the healthy doctrine on Purgatory, transmitted by the Holy Fathers and the Sacred Councils, be believed by the Christian faithful, be kept, taught and preached everywhere.

Moreover, the Bishops must take care that the suffrages of the faithful, namely, the sacrifices of Masses, prayers, alms and other works of piety, which are usually undertaken for the deceased, be carried out piously and devoutly as established by the Church and that she satisfy with indulgence and exactitude, all that must be done for the deceased as exacted by the foundations of the testators, or other reasons, not superficially but by priests and ministers of the Church and others that have this obligation.'

Canon 30, session 6 of January 13, 1547, states: 'If someone rejects temporal punishment in this life or the next, after having been absolved, let him be accursed.'

In chapter 9 of November 25, 1551, the Council certifies that before the Heavenly Father, through Jesus, we begin first to repair temporal punishment with the penance imposed by the priest, according to the level of our offense and then we repair with the love with which we received all the trials we experience in this life.

In session 25 of December 4, 1563, the Church established as dogma the **existence of Purgatory.**

In session 14 the same Council certified the fact that our sins are forgiven, first in the Blood of Christ and second in the Sacrament of Reconciliation - established by Christ himself through his Apostles - man is not exempt from the consequences of sin, namely, from temporal punishment. This means that, if man does not do reparation for the sin forgiven during his earthly life, he will have to be purified and pay the punishment in the temporal prison, namely, in Purgatory. It is also a dogma of the Church that our prayers as Militant Church, especially the Masses offered for the dead, benefit the souls in Purgatory.

After the Council of Trent, the Ecclesiastical Magisterium took the following decision:

Pius IV's profession of faith in 1564: 'I hold constantly as certain that there is a Purgatory, that the souls detained there are helped by the suffrages of the faithful.'

Pius IV's condemnation of proposition 42 of the Jansenist Synod of Pistoya which declared illusory the application of indulgences to the deceased.[5]

VII. VATICAN COUNCIL II

Dogmatic Constitution *Lumen Gentium* No. 49

Communion of the Heavenly Church with the Pilgrim Church

49. 'Until the Lord shall come in His majesty, and all the angels with Him (cf. *Matthew* 25:3) and death being destroyed, all things are subject to Him,((cf. 1 *Corinthians* 15:26-27) some of His disciples are exiles on earth, some having died are purified,

---

5   *"Catholic.net – Council of Trent. Years 1545-1563."* N.p., n.d. Web. 02 Apr. 2013.

and others are in glory beholding "clearly God Himself Triune and one, as He is"; but all in various ways and degrees are in communion in the same charity of God and neighbor and all sing the same hymn of glory to our God. For all who are in Christ, having His Spirit, form one Church and cleave together in Him.(cf. *Ephesians* 4:16) Therefore the union of the wayfarers with the brethren who have gone to sleep in the peace of Christ is not in the least weakened or interrupted, but on the contrary, according to the perpetual faith of the Church, is strengthened by communication of spiritual goods. For by reason of the fact that those in heaven are more closely united with Christ, they establish the whole Church more firmly in holiness, lend nobility to the worship which the Church offers to God here on earth and in many ways contribute to its greater edification.(cf. 1 *Corinthians* 12:12-27) For after they have been received into their heavenly home and are present to the Lord, (cf. 2 *Corinthians* 5:8) through Him and with Him and in Him they do not cease to intercede with the Father for us, showing forth the merits which they won on earth through the one Mediator between God and man, (1 *Timothy* 2:5) serving God in all things and filling up in their flesh those things which are lacking of the sufferings of Christ for His Body which is the Church.(cf. *Colossians* 1:24)Thus by their brotherly interest our weakness is greatly strengthened.'

Relations of the Pilgrim Church with the Heavenly Church

50. 'Fully conscious of this communion of the whole Mystical Body of Jesus Christ, the pilgrim Church from the very first ages of the Christian religion has cultivated with great piety the memory of the dead, and "because it is a holy and wholesome

thought to pray for the dead that they may be loosed from their sins",(2 *Maccabees* 12:46) also offers suffrages for them.

The Church has always believed that the apostles and Christ's martyrs, who had given the supreme witness of faith and charity by the shedding of their blood, are closely joined with us in Christ, and she has always venerated them with special devotion, together with the Blessed Virgin Mary and the holy angels. The Church has piously implored the aid of their intercession. To these were soon added also those who had more closely imitated Christ's virginity and poverty, and finally others whom the outstanding practice of the Christian virtues and the divine charisms recommended to the pious devotion and imitation of the faithful.

When we look at the lives of those who have faithfully followed Christ, we are inspired with a new reason for seeking the City that is to come (cf. *Hebrews* 11:10; 13-1) and at the same time we are shown a most safe path by which, among the vicissitudes of this world, in keeping with the state in life and condition proper to each of us, we will be able to arrive at perfect union with Christ, that is, perfect holiness. In the lives of those who, sharing in our humanity, are however more perfectly transformed into the image of Christ, (cf. 2 *Corinthians* 3:18) God vividly manifests His presence and His face to men. He speaks to us in them, and gives us a sign of His Kingdom, to which we are strongly drawn, having so great a cloud of witnesses over us (cf. *Hebrews* 12:1) and such a witness to the truth of the Gospel.

Nor is it by the title of example only, that we cherish the memory of those in heaven, but still more in order that the union of the whole Church may be strengthened in the Spirit by the practice of fraternal charity.(cf. *Ephesians* 4:1-6) For just as Christian communion among wayfarers brings us closer to Christ, so our companionship with the saints joins us to Christ, from Whom as from its Fountain and Head issues every grace and the very life of the people of God. It is supremely fitting, therefore, that we love those friends and coheirs of Jesus Christ, who are also our brothers and extraordinary benefactors, that we render due thanks to God for them and "suppliantly invoke them and have recourse to their prayers, their power and help in obtaining benefits from God through His Son, Jesus Christ, who is our Redeemer and Savior."

For every genuine testimony of love shown by us to those in heaven, by its very nature tends toward and terminates in Christ who is the "crown of all saints", and through Him, in God Who is wonderful in his saints and is magnified in them.

Our union with the Church in heaven is put into effect in its noblest manner especially in the sacred Liturgy, wherein the power of the Holy Spirit acts upon us through sacramental signs. Then, with combined rejoicing we celebrate together the praise of the divine majesty; then all those from every tribe and tongue and people and nation (cf. *Revelation* 5:9) who have been redeemed by the blood of Christ and gathered together into one Church, with one song of praise magnify the One and Triune God.

Celebrating the Eucharistic sacrifice therefore, we are most closely united to the Church in heaven in communion with and venerating the memory first of all of the glorious ever-Virgin

Mary, of Blessed Joseph and the blessed apostles and martyrs and of all the saints.'

The Council Establishes Pastoral Dispositions

51. 'This Sacred Council accepts with great devotion this venerable faith of our ancestors regarding this vital fellowship with our brethren who are in heavenly glory or who having died are still being purified; and it proposes again the decrees of the Second Council of Nicaea, the Council of Florence and the Council of Trent. And at the same time, in conformity with our own pastoral interests, we urge all concerned, if any abuses, excesses or defects have crept in here or there, to do what is in their power to remove or correct them, and to restore all things to a fuller praise of Christ and of God. Let them therefore teach the faithful that the authentic cult of the saints consists not so much in the multiplying of external acts, but rather in the greater intensity of our love, whereby, for our own greater good and that of the whole Church, we seek from the saints "example in their way of life, fellowship in their communion, and aid by their intercession." On the other hand, let them teach the faithful that our communion with those in heaven, provided that it is understood in the fuller light of faith according to its genuine nature, in no way weakens, but conversely, more thoroughly enriches the latreutic worship we give to God the Father, through Christ, in the Spirit.

For all of us, who are sons of God and constitute one family in Christ,(cf. *Hebrews* 3:6) as long as we remain in communion with one another in mutual charity and in one praise of the most holy Trinity, are corresponding with the intimate vocation of the Church and partaking in foretaste the liturgy of consummate glory. For when Christ shall appear and the glorious resurrection of the dead will take place, the glory of God will light up the heavenly City and the Lamb will be the lamp thereof.(cf. *Revelation* 21-24) Then the whole Church of the saints in the supreme happiness of charity will adore God and "the Lamb who was slain",(*Revelation* 5:12) proclaiming with one voice: "To Him who sits upon the throne, and to the Lamb blessing, and honor, and glory, and dominion forever and ever." ' (*Revelation* 5:13).[6]

B. CATECHISM OF THE CATHOLIC CHURCH

The Catechism is built upon what Scripture proclaims about Purgatory. It forms part of what the Church calls the *Novisimos*, that is: Death. Judgment, Purgatory, Heaven and Hell.

Here is what it sets forth:

1030. 'All who die in God's grace and friendship, but still imperfectly purified, are indeed assured of their eternal salvation; but after death they undergo purification, so as to achieve the holiness necessary to enter the joy of Heaven.'

1031. 'The Church gives the name *Purgatory* to this final purification of the elect, which is entirely different from the punishment of the damned. The Church formulated her doctrine of faith on Purgatory especially in the Councils of Florence (cf. DS 1304) and Trent (cf. DS 1820; 1580). The

6   *"Dogmatic Constitution Lumen Gentium on the Church."* N.p., n.d. Web. 02 Apr. 2013.

tradition of the Church, by reference to certain texts of Scripture, speaks of a cleansing fire.

As for lesser faults, we must believe that, before the Final Judgment, there is a purifying fire. He who is Truth says that whoever utters blasphemy against the Holy Spirit will be pardoned neither in this age nor in the age to come. From this sentence we understand that certain offenses can be forgiven in this age, but certain others in the age to come'. (Saint Gregory the Great, *Dialogues* 4, 39).

Aid to Souls in Purgatory

1032. 'This teaching is also based on the practice of prayer for the dead, already mentioned in Sacred Scripture: "Therefore [Judas Maccabeus] made atonement for the dead, that they might be delivered from their sin" (2 *Maccabees* 12:46). From the beginning the Church has honored the memory of the dead and offered prayers in suffrage for them, above all the Eucharistic sacrifice (cf. DS 856), so that, thus purified, they may attain the beatific vision of God. The Church also commends almsgiving, indulgences and works of penance undertaken on behalf of the dead:

"Let us help and commemorate them. If Job's sons were purified by their father's sacrifice (cf. *Job* 1:5), why would we doubt that our offerings for the dead bring them some consolation? Let us not hesitate to help those who have died and to offer our prayers for them" ' (Saint John Chrysostom, *In epistulam I ad Corinthios,* homily in 1 *Corinthians* 41:5).

Prayers

958. *'Communion with the Dead.* In full consciousness of this communion of the whole Mystical Body of Jesus Christ, the Church in its pilgrim members, from the very earliest days of the Christian religion, has honored with great respect the memory of the dead; and "because it is a holy and a wholesome thought to pray for the dead that they may be loosed from their sins" she offers her suffrages for them (2 *Maccabees* 12:45) (LG 50). Our prayer for them is capable not only of helping them, but also of making their intercession for us effective.'

Eucharistic Sacrifice

1371. ' The Eucharistic sacrifice is also offered for *the faithful departed* who "have died in Christ but are not yet wholly purified" (Cc. of Trent: DS 1743), so that they may be able to enter into the light and peace of Christ:

"Lay this body wherever it may be. Let no care of it disturb you: this only I ask of you that you should remember me at the altar of the Lord". (Saint Augustine, *Confessions* 9, 11, 27; words of Saint Monica, addressed to Saint Augustine and his brother before her death).

'Then we pray (in the anaphora) for the holy Fathers and Bishops who have fallen asleep, and in general for all who have fallen asleep before us, in the belief that it is a great benefit to the souls on whose behalf the supplication is offered, while the holy and tremendous Victim is present [...] By offering to God our supplications for those who have fallen asleep, if they have sinned, we [...] offer Christ sacrifice for the sins of all, and so render favorable, for them and for us, the God who loves man' (Saint Cyril of Jerusalem, *Catecheses mistagogicae* 5, 9.10).

C. BIBLICAL FOUNDATION

OLD TESTAMENT

2 Maccabees 12:42-46:

'They gave themselves to prayer, begging that the sin which had been committed might be wholly blotted out. And the noble Judas exhorted the people to keep themselves free from sin, for they had seen with their own eyes what had happened because of the sin of those who had fallen. He also took up a collection man by man, to the amount of two thousand drachmas of silver, and sent it to Jerusalem to provide for a sin offering. In doing this he acted very well and honorably, taking account of the resurrection. For if he were not expecting that those who had fallen would rise again, it would have been superfluous and foolish to pray for the dead.

But if he was looking to the splendid reward that is laid up for those who fall asleep in godliness, it was a holy and pious thought. Therefore he made atonement for the dead, so that they might be delivered from their sin.'

Micah 7:8-9:

'Rejoice not against me, O my enemy: when I fall, I shall rise; when I sit in darkness, the Lord shall be a light to me, I will bear the indignation of the Lord, because I have sinned against him, until he pleads my cause, and executes judgment for me. He will bring me forth to the light and I shall behold his righteousness.'

NEW TESTAMENT

Matthew 12:32

'And whoever says a word against the Son of man will be forgiven; but whoever speaks against the Holy Spirit will not be forgiven, either in this age or in the age to come.'

Matthew 18:34-35

'And in anger his lord delivered him to the jailers, till he should pay all his debt. So also my heavenly Father will do to every one of you, if you do not forgive your brother from your heart.'

1 Corinthians 3:14-15

'If the work which any man has built on the foundation survives, he will receive a reward. If any man's work is burned up, he will suffer loss, though he himself will be saved, but only as through fire.'[7]

---

7   *Bible of Navarre.* Popular Edition. EUNSA

D. CATECHESIS OF SAINT JOHN PAUL II ON PURGATORY

GENERAL AUDIENCE

Wednesday, August 4, 1999

1. ' As we have seen in the previous two catechesis, on the basis of the definitive option for or against God, the human being finds he faces one of these alternatives: either to live with the Lord in eternal beatitude, or to remain far from his presence.

For those who find themselves in a condition of being open to God, but still imperfectly, the journey towards full beatitude requires a purification, which the faith of the Church illustrates in the doctrine of "Purgatory" (cf. Catechism of the Catholic Church, n. 1030-1032).

2. In Sacred Scripture, we can grasp certain elements that help us to understand the meaning of this doctrine, even if it is not formally described. They express the belief that we cannot approach God without undergoing some kind of purification.

According to Old Testament religious law, what is destined for God must be perfect. As a result, physical integrity is also specifically required for the realities which come into contact with God at the sacrificial level such as, for example, sacrificial animals (cf. Leviticus 22:22) or at the institutional level, as in the case of priests or ministers of worship (cf. Leviticus 21:17-23). Total dedication to the God of the Covenant, along the lines of the great teachings found in Deuteronomy (cf. 6:5), and which must correspond to this physical integrity, is required of individuals and society as a whole (cf. 1 Kgs8:61).

It is a matter of loving God with all one's being, with purity of heart and the witness of deeds (cf. Ibid., 10:12f.).

The need for integrity obviously becomes necessary after death, for entering into perfect and complete communion with God. Those who do not possess this integrity must undergo purification. This is suggested by a text of Saint Paul.

The Apostle speaks of the value of each person's work which will be revealed on the day of judgment and says: "If the work which any man has built on the foundation [which is Christ] survives, he will receive a reward. If any man's work is burned up, he will suffer loss, though he himself will be saved, but only as through fire" (1 Corinthians 3:14-15).

3. At times, to reach a state of perfect integrity a person's intercession or mediation is needed. For example, Moses obtains pardon for the people with a prayer in which he recalls the saving work done by God in the past, and prays for God's fidelity to the oath made to his ancestors (cf. Ex 32:30, 11-13).

The figure of the Servant of the Lord, outlined in the Book of Isaiah, is also portrayed by his role of intercession and expiation for many; at the end of his suffering he "will see the light" and "will justify many", bearing their iniquities (cf. Isaiah 52:13-53, 12, especially vv. 53:11).

Psalm 51 can be considered, according to the perspective of the Old Testament, as a synthesis of the process of reintegration: the sinner confesses and recognizes his guilt (v. 3), asking insistently to be purified or "cleansed" (vv. 2, 9, 10, 17) so as to proclaim the divine praise (v. 15).

4. In the New Testament Christ is presented as the intercessor who assumes the functions of high priest on the day of expiation (cf. Hebrews 5:7; 7:25). But in him the priesthood is presented in a new and definitive form.

He enters the heavenly shrine once and for all, to intercede with God on our behalf (cf. Hebrews 9:23-26, especially, v. 24). He is both priest and "victim of expiation" for the sins of the whole world (cf. 1 John 2:2).

Jesus, as the great intercessor who atones for us, will fully reveal himself at the end of our life when he will express himself with the offer of mercy, but also with the inevitable judgment for those who refuse the Father's love and forgiveness. This offer of mercy does not exclude the duty to present ourselves to God, pure and whole, rich in that love which Paul calls a "[bond] of perfect harmony" (Colossians 3:14).

5. In following the Gospel exhortation to be perfect like the heavenly Father (cf. Matthew 5:48) during our earthly life, we are called to grow in love, to be sound and flawless before God the Father "at the coming of our Lord Jesus with all his saints" (1 Thessalonians 3:12f.). Moreover, we are invited to "cleanse ourselves from every defilement of body and spirit" (2 Corinthians 7:1; cf. 1 John 3:3), because the encounter with God requires absolute purity.

Every trace of attachment to evil must be eliminated, every imperfection of the soul corrected. Purification must be complete, and indeed this is precisely what is meant by the Church's teaching on Purgatory. The term does not indicate a place, but a condition of existence.

Those who, after death, exist in a state of purification are already in the love of Christ who removes from them the remnants of imperfection (cf. Ecumenical Council of Florence, Decretum pro Graecis: DS 1304; Ecumenical Council of Trent, Decretum de iustificatione: DS 1580; Decretum de purgatorio: DS 1820).

It is necessary to explain that the state of purification is not a prolongation of the earthly condition, almost as if after death one were given another possibility to change one's destiny. The Church's teaching in this regard is unequivocal and was reaffirmed by the Second Vatican Council which teaches: "Since we know neither the day nor the hour, we should follow the advice of the Lord and watch constantly so that, when the single course of our earthly life is completed (cf. Hebrews 9:27), we may merit to enter with him into the marriage feast and be numbered among the blessed, and not, like the wicked and slothful servants, be ordered to depart into the eternal fire, into the outer darkness where " men will weep and gnash their teeth " (Matthew 22:13 and 25:30) (Lumen Gentium, n. 48).

6. One last important aspect which the Church's tradition has always pointed out should be re-proposed today: the dimension of 'communio'. Those, in fact, who find themselves in the state of purification are united both with the blessed who

already enjoy the fullness of eternal life, and with us on this earth on our way towards the Father's house (cf. CCC, n. 1032).

Just as in their earthly life believers are united in the one Mystical Body, so after death those who live in a state of purification experience the same ecclesial solidarity which works through prayer, prayers for suffrage and love for their other brothers and sisters in the faith. Purification is lived in the essential bond created between those who live in this world and those who enjoy eternal beatitude.'[8]

E. CATECHESIS OF HIS HOLINESS POPE BENEDICT XVI ON PURGATORY

The Holy Father Benedict XVI spoke expressly about Purgatory in his encyclical letter Spe Salvi.

Judgment as a Setting for Learning and Practicing Hope

41. 'At the conclusion of the central section of the Church's great Credo – the part that recounts the mystery of Christ, from his eternal birth of the Father and his temporal birth of the Virgin Mary, through his Cross and Resurrection to the second coming – we find the phrase: "he will come again in glory to judge the living and the dead". From the earliest times, the prospect of the Judgment has influenced Christians in their daily living as a criterion by which to order their present life, as a summons to their conscience, and at the same time as hope in God's justice.

---

8   John Paul II. "August 4, 1999, *Purgatory.*" N.p., n.d.

Faith in Christ has never looked merely backwards or merely upwards, but always also forwards to the hour of justice
that the Lord repeatedly proclaimed. This looking ahead has
given Christianity its importance for the present moment. In
the arrangement of Christian sacred buildings, which were
intended to make visible the historic and cosmic breadth of
faith in Christ, it became customary to depict the Lord returning as a king – the symbol of hope – at the east end;
while the west wall normally portrayed the Last Judgment as
a symbol of our responsibility for our lives – a scene which
followed and accompanied the faithful as they went out to
resume their daily routine. As the iconography of the Last
Judgment developed, however, more and more prominence
was given to its ominous and frightening aspects, which obviously held more fascination for artists than the splendor of
hope, often all too well concealed beneath the horrors.

42. In the modern era, the idea of the Last Judgment has
faded into the background: Christian faith has been individu-
alised and primarily oriented towards the salvation of the believer's own soul, while reflection on world history is largely
dominated by the idea of progress. The fundamental content
of awaiting a final Judgment, however, has not disappeared:
it has simply taken on a totally different form.

The atheism of the nineteenth and twentieth centuries is
– in its origins and aims – a type of moralism: a protest
against the injustices of the world and of world history.
A world marked by so much injustice, innocent suffering,
and cynicism of power cannot be the work of a good
God. A God with responsibility for such a world would
not be a just God, much less a good God.

It is for the sake of morality that this God has to be contested. Since there is no God to create justice, it seems man himself is now called to establish justice. If in the face of this world's suffering, protest against God is understandable, the claim that humanity can and must do what no God actually does or is able to do is both presumptuous and intrinsically false. It is no accident that this idea has led to the greatest forms of cruelty and violations of justice; rather, it is grounded in the intrinsic falsity of the claim. A world which has to create its own justice is a world without hope. No one and nothing can answer for centuries of suffering. No one and nothing can guarantee that the cynicism of power – whatever beguiling ideological mask it adopts – will cease to dominate the world. This is why the great thinkers of the Frankfurt School, Max Horkheimer and Theodor W. Adorno, were equally critical of atheism and theism. Horkheimer radically excluded the possibility of ever finding a this-worldly substitute for God, while at the same time he rejected the image of a good and just God.

In an extreme radicalisation of the Old Testament prohibition of images, he speaks of a "longing for the totally Other" that remains inaccessible – a cry of yearning directed at world history. Adorno also firmly upheld this total rejection of images, which naturally meant the exclusion of any "image" of a loving God. On the other hand, he also constantly emphasised this "negative" dialectic and asserted that justice – true justice – would require a world "where not only present suffering would be wiped out, but also that which is irrevocably past would be undone"[30]. This, would mean, however – to express it with positive and hence, for him, inadequate symbols – that there can be no justice without a resurrection of the dead. Yet this would have to involve "the resurrection of the flesh, something that is totally foreign to idealism and the realm of Absolute spirit"[31].

43. Christians likewise can and must constantly learn from the strict rejection of images that is contained in God's first commandment (cf. *Ex* 20:4). The truth of negative theology was highlighted by the Fourth Lateran Council, which explicitly stated that however great the similarity that may be established between Creator and creature, the dissimilarity between them is always greater [32]. In any case, for the believer the rejection of images cannot be carried so far that one ends up, as Horkheimer and Adorno would like, by saying "no" to both theses – theism and atheism. God has given himself an "image": in Christ who was made man. In him who was crucified, the denial of false images of God is taken to an extreme. God now reveals his true face in the figure of the sufferer who shares man's God-forsaken condition by taking it upon himself.

This innocent sufferer has attained the certitude of hope: there is a God, and God can create justice in a way that we cannot conceive, yet we can begin to grasp it through faith. Yes, there is a resurrection of the flesh [33]. There is justice [34]. There is an "undoing" of past suffering, a reparation that sets things aright. For this reason, faith in the Last Judgment is first and foremost hope – the need for which was made abundantly clear in the upheavals of recent centuries.

I am convinced that the question of justice constitutes the essential argument, or in any case the strongest argument, in favor of faith in eternal life. The purely individual need for a fulfilment that is denied to us in this life, for an everlasting love that we await, is certainly an important motive for believing that man was made for eternity; but only in connection with the impossibility that the injustice of history should be the final word does the necessity for Christ's return and for new life become fully convincing.

44. To protest against God in the name of justice is not helpful. A world without God is a world without hope (cf. *Ephesians* 2:12). Only God can create justice. And faith gives us the certainty that he does so. The image of the Last Judgment is not primarily an image of terror, but an image of hope; for us it may even be the decisive image of hope. Is it not also a frightening image? I would say: it is an image that evokes responsibility, an image, therefore, of that fear of which Saint Hilary spoke when he said that all our fear has its place in love [35].

God is justice and creates justice. This is our consolation and our hope. And in his justice there is also grace. This we know by turning our gaze to the crucified and risen Christ. Both these things – justice and grace – must be seen in their correct inner relationship.

Grace does not cancel out justice. It does not make wrong into right. It is not a sponge which wipes everything away, so that whatever someone has done on earth ends up being of equal value. Dostoevsky, for example, was right to protest against this kind of Heaven and this kind of grace in his novel The Brothers Karamazov. Evildoers, in the end, do not sit at table at the eternal banquet beside their victims without distinction, as though nothing had happened.

Here I would like to quote a passage from Plato which expresses a premonition of just judgment that in many respects remains true and salutary for Christians too. Albeit using mythological images, he expresses the truth with an unambiguous clarity, saying that in the end souls will stand naked before the judge. It no longer matters what they once were in history, but only what they are in truth: "Often, when it is the king or some other monarch or potentate that he (the judge) has to deal with, he finds that there is no soundness in the soul whatever; he finds it scourged and scarred by the various acts of perjury and wrong-doing [...] ; it is twisted and warped by lies and vanity, and nothing is straight because truth has had no part in its development. Power, luxury, pride, and debauchery have left it so full of disproportion and ugliness that when he has inspected it (he) sends it straight to prison, where on its arrival it will undergo the appropriate punishment [...] Sometimes, though, the eye of the judge lights on a different soul which has lived in purity and truth [...] then he is struck with admiration and sends him to the isles of the blessed" [36].

In the parable of the rich man and Lazarus (cf. *Luke* 16:19-31), Jesus admonishes us through the image of a soul destroyed by arrogance and opulence, who has created an impassable chasm between himself and the poor man; the chasm of being trapped within material pleasures; the chasm of forgetting the other, of incapacity to love, which then becomes a burning and unquenchable thirst. We must note that in this parable Jesus is not referring to the final destiny after the Last Judgment, but is taking up a notion found, *inter alia*, in early Judaism, namely that of an intermediate state between death and resurrection, a state in which the final sentence is yet to be pronounced.

45. This early Jewish idea of an intermediate state includes the view that these souls are not simply in a sort of temporary custody but, as the parable of the rich man illustrates, are already being punished or are experiencing a provisional form of bliss. There is also the idea that this state can involve purification and healing which mature the soul for communion with God.

The early Church took up these concepts, and in the Western Church they gradually developed into the doctrine of Purgatory. We do not need to examine here the complex historical paths of this development; it is enough to ask what it actually means. With death, our life-choice becomes definitive — our life stands before the judge. Our choice, which in the course of an entire life takes on a certain shape, can have a variety of forms.

There can be people who have totally destroyed their desire for truth and readiness to love, people for whom everything has become a lie, people who have lived for hatred and have suppressed all love within themselves. This is a terrifying thought, but alarming profiles of this type can be seen in certain figures of our own history. In such people all would be beyond remedy and the destruction of good would be irrevocable: this is what we mean by the word Hell [37]. On the other hand there can be people who are utterly pure, completely permeated by God, and thus fully open to their neighbors — people for whom communion with God even now gives direction to their entire being and whose journey towards God only brings to fulfilment what they already are [38].

46. Yet we know from experience that neither case is normal in human life. For the great majority of people — we may suppose — there remains in the depths of their being an ultimate interior openness to truth, to love, to God. In the concrete choices of life, however, it is covered over by ever new compromises with evil — much filth covers purity, but the thirst for purity remains and it still constantly re-emerges from all that is base and remains present in the soul.

What happens to such individuals when they appear before the Judge? Will all the impurity they have amassed through life suddenly cease to matter? What else might occur? Saint Paul, in his First Letter to the Corinthians, gives us an idea of the differing impact of God's judgment according to each person's particular circumstances. He does this using images which in some way try to express the invisible, without it being possible for us to conceptualise these images — simply because we can neither see into the world beyond death nor do we have any experience of it.

Paul begins by saying that Christian life is built upon a common foundation: Jesus Christ. This foundation endures. If we have stood firm on this foundation and built our life upon it, we know that it cannot be taken away from us even in death. Then Paul continues: "Now if any one builds on the foundation with gold, silver, precious stones, wood, hay, straw — each man's work will become manifest; for the Day will disclose it, because it will be revealed with fire, and the fire will test what sort of work each one has done. If the work which any man has built on the foundation survives, he will receive a reward. If any man's work is burned up, he will suffer loss, though he himself will be saved, but only as through fire" (1 Cor 3:12-15).

In this text, it is in any case evident that our salvation can take different forms, that some of what is built may be burned down, that in order to be saved we personally have to pass through "fire" so as to become fully open to receiving God and able to take our place at the table of the eternal marriage-feast.

47. Some recent theologians are of the opinion that the fire which both burns and saves is Christ himself, the Judge and Savior. The encounter with him is the decisive act of judgment. Before his gaze all falsehood melts away. This encounter with him, as it burns us, transforms and frees us, allowing us to become truly ourselves. All that we build during our lives can prove to be mere straw, pure bluster, and it collapses. Yet in the pain of this encounter, when the impurity and sickness of our lives become evident to us, there lies salvation. His gaze, the touch of his heart heals us through an undeniably painful transformation "as through fire". But it is a blessed pain, in which the holy power of his love sears through us like a flame, enabling us to become totally ourselves and thus totally of God. In this way the inter-relation between justice and grace also becomes clear: the way we live our lives is not immaterial, but our defilement does not stain us for ever if we have at least continued to reach out towards Christ, towards truth and towards love. Indeed, it has already been burned away through Christ's Passion.

At the moment of judgment we experience and we absorb the overwhelming power of his love over all the evil in the world and in ourselves. The pain of love becomes our salvation and our joy. It is clear that we cannot calculate the "duration" of this transforming burning in terms of the chronological measurements of this world. The transforming "moment" of this encounter eludes earthly time-reckoning — it is the heart's time, it is the time of "passage" to communion with God in the Body of Christ [39].

The judgment of God is hope, both because it is justice and because it is grace. If it were merely grace, making all earthly things cease to matter, God would still owe us an answer to the question about justice — the crucial question that we ask of history and of God. If it were merely justice, in the end it could bring only fear to us all. The incarnation of God in Christ has so closely linked the two together—judgment and grace— that justice is firmly established: we all work out our salvation 'with fear and trembling' (Philippians 2:12). Nevertheless grace allows us all to hope, and to go trustfully to meet the Judge whom we know as our 'advocate', or *parakletos* (cf. 1 John 2:1).

48. A further point must be mentioned here, because it is important for the practice of Christian hope. Early Jewish thought includes the idea that one can help the deceased in their intermediate state through prayer (see for example *2 Maccabees* 12:38-45; first century BC). The equivalent practice was readily adopted by Christians and is common to the Eastern and Western Church. The East does not recognise the purifying and expiatory suffering of souls in the afterlife, but it does acknowledge various levels of beatitude and of suffering in the intermediate state.

The souls of the departed can, however, receive "solace and refreshment" through the Eucharist, prayer and almsgiving. The belief that love can reach into the afterlife, that reciprocal giving and receiving is possible, in which our affection for one another continues beyond the limits of death – this has been a fundamental conviction of Christianity throughout the ages and it remains a source of comfort today.

Who would not feel the need to convey to their departed loved ones a sign of kindness, a gesture of gratitude or even a request for pardon? Now a further question arises: if 'Purgatory' is simply purification through fire in the encounter with the Lord, Judge and Savior, how can a third person intervene, even if he or she is particularly close to the other? When we ask such a question, we should recall that no man is an island, entire of itself. Our lives are involved with one another, through innumerable interactions they are linked together. No one lives alone. No one sins alone. No one is saved alone. The lives of others continually spill over into mine: in what I think, say, do and achieve. And conversely, my life spills over into that of others: for better and for worse. So my prayer for another is not something extraneous to that person, something external, not even after death.

In the interconnectedness of Being, my gratitude to the other – my prayer for him – can play a small part in his purification. And for that there is no need to convert earthly time into God's time: in the communion of souls simple terrestrial time is superseded. It is never too late to touch the heart of another, nor is it ever in vain.

In this way we further clarify an important element of the Christian concept of hope. Our hope is always essentially also hope for others; only thus is it truly hope for me too [40]. As Christians we should never limit ourselves to asking: how can I save myself? We should also ask: what can I do in order that others may be saved and that for them too the star of hope may rise? Then I will have done my utmost for my own personal salvation as well."[9]

In a General Audience, the Holy Father Benedict XVI gave a catechesis in Paul VI Hall to a group of faithful and pilgrims from Italy and the whole world, in which he referred to the life of Saint Catherine of Genoa and to Purgatory.

Vatican City, Wednesday, January 12, 2011

'Dear Brothers and Sisters:

Today I would like to speak about another Saint who, as Catherine of Siena and Catherine of Bologna, is also called Catherine. I am speaking of Catherine of Genoa, who is distinguished especially for her visions of Purgatory.

The text that tells us about her life and thought was published in the city of Ligure in 1551. It is divided in three parts: her Life as such, the Demonstration and Declaration of Purgatory -- better known as Treatise -- and the Dialogue between the Soul and the Body. The compiler of Catherine's work was her confessor, the priest Cattaneo Marabotto.

Catherine was born in Genoa in 1447. She was the youngest of five. Her Father, Giacomo Fieschi, died when she was very young. Her mother, Francesca di Negro provided such an effective Christian education that the elder of her two daughters became a religious. When Catherine was 16, she

---

9   *Spe Salvi* -- Encyclical Letter, Benedict XVI. N.p., n.d. Web.

was given in marriage to Giuliano Adorno, a man who after various trading and military experiences in the Middle East, had returned to Genoa in order to marry.

Married life was far from easy for Catherine, partly because of the character of her husband who was given to gambling. Catherine herself was at first induced to lead a worldly sort of life in which, however, she failed to find serenity. After 10 years, her heart was heavy with a deep sense of emptiness and bitterness.

A unique experience on 20 March 1473 sparked her conversion. She had gone to the Church of San Benedetto in the monastery of Nostra Signora delle Grazie [Our Lady of Grace], to make her confession and, kneeling before the priest, 'received,' as she herself wrote, "a wound in my heart from God's immense love." It came with such a clear vision of her own wretchedness and shortcomings, and at the same time of God's goodness, that she almost fainted.

Her heart was moved by this knowledge of herself – knowledge of the empty life she was leading and of the goodness of God. This experience prompted the decision that gave direction to her whole life. She expressed it in the words: "no longer the world, no longer sin" (cf. Vita mirabile, 3rv). Catherine did not stay to make her Confession.

On arriving home she entered the remotest room and spent a long time weeping. At that moment she received an inner instruction on prayer and became aware of God's immense love for her, a sinner. It was a spiritual experience she had not words to describe (cf. Vita mirabile, 4r).

It was on this occasion that the suffering Jesus appeared to her, bent beneath the Cross, as he is often portrayed in the Saint's iconography. A few days later she returned to the priest to make a good confession at last. It was here that began the "life of purification" which for many years caused her to feel constant sorrow for the sins she had committed and which spurred her to impose forms of penance and sacrifice upon herself, in order to show her love to God.

On this journey, Catherine became ever closer to the Lord until she attained what is called "unitive life," namely, a relationship of profound union with God.

In her Vita it is written that her soul was guided and instructed from within solely by the sweet love of God which gave her all she needed. Catherine surrendered herself so totally into the hands of the Lord that she lived, for about 25 years, as she wrote, "without the assistance of any creature, taught and governed by God alone" (Vita, 117r-118r), nourished above all by constant prayer and by Holy Communion which she received every day, an unusual practice in her time. Only many years later did the Lord give her a priest who cared for her soul.

Catherine was always reluctant to confide and reveal her experience of mystical communion with God, especially because of the deep humility she felt before the Lord's graces. The prospect of glorifying him and of being able to contribute to the spiritual journey of others alone spurred her to recount what had taken place within her, from the moment of her conversion, which is her original and fundamental experience.

The place of her ascent to mystical peaks was Pammatone Hospital, the largest hospital complex in Genoa, of which she was director and animator. Hence Catherine lived a totally active existence despite the depth of her inner life. In Pammatone a group of followers, disciples and collaborators formed around her, fascinated by her life of faith and her charity.

Indeed her husband, Giuliano Adorno, was so won over that he gave up his dissipated life, became a Third Order Franciscan and moved into the hospital to help his wife.

Catherine's dedication to caring for the sick continued until the end of her earthly life on 15 September 1510. From her conversion until her death there were no extraordinary events but two elements characterise her entire life: one the one hand her mystical experience, that is, the profound union with God, which she felt As spousal union, and on the other, assistance to the sick, the organisation of the hospital and service to her neighbor, especially the neediest and the most forsaken. These two poles, God and neighbor, totally filled her life, virtually all of which she spent within the hospital walls.

Dear friends, we must never forget that the more we love God and the more constantly we pray, the better we will succeed in truly loving those who surround us, who are close to us, so that we can see in every person the Face of the Lord whose love knows no bounds and makes no distinctions. The mystic does not create distance from others or an abstract life, but rather approaches other people so that they may begin to see and act with God's eyes and heart.

Catherine's thought on Purgatory, for which she is particularly well known, is summed up in the last two parts of the book mentioned above: The Treatise on Purgatory and the Dialogues between the Body and the Soul. It is important to note that Catherine, in her mystical experience, never received specific revelations on purgatory or on the souls being purified there. Yet, in the writings inspired by our Saint, purgatory is a central element and the description of it has characteristics that were original in her time.

The first original passage concerns the "place" of the purification of souls. In her day it was depicted mainly using images linked to space: a certain space was conceived of in which Purgatory was supposed to be located.

Catherine, however, did not see purgatory as a scene in the bowels of the earth: for her it is not an exterior but rather an interior fire. This is Purgatory: an inner fire. The Saint speaks of the Soul's journey of purification on the way to full communion with God, starting from her own experience of profound sorrow for the sins committed, in comparison with God's infinite love (cf. Vita mirabile, 171v).

We heard of the moment of conversion when Catherine suddenly became aware of God's goodness, of the infinite distance of her own life from this goodness and of a burning fire within her. And this is the fire that purifies, the interior fire of purgatory. Here too is an original feature in comparison with the thought of her time.

In fact, she does not start with the afterlife in order to recount the torments of purgatory – as was the custom in her time and perhaps still is today – and then to point out the way to purification or conversion. Rather our Saint begins with the inner experience of her own life on the way to Eternity.

"The soul", Catherine says, "presents itself to God still bound to the desires and suffering that derive from sin and this makes it impossible for it to enjoy the beatific vision of God." Catherine asserts that God is so pure and holy that a soul stained by sin cannot be in the presence of the divine majesty (cf. Vita mirabile, 177r).

We too feel how distant we are, how full we are of so many things that we cannot see God. The soul is aware of the immense love and perfect justice of God and consequently suffers for having failed to respond in a correct and perfect way to this love; and love for God itself becomes a flame; love itself cleanses it from the residue of sin.

In Catherine we can make out the presence of theological and mystical sources on which it was normal to draw in her time. In particular, we find an image of Dionysius the Areopagite: the thread of gold that links the human heart to God himself. When God purified man, he bound him with the finest golden thread, that is, his love, and draws him toward himself with such strong affection that man is as it were "overcome and won over and completely beside himself."

Thus the human heart is pervaded by God's love that becomes the one guide, the one driving force of his life (cf. Vita mirabile, 246rv). This situation of being uplifted towards God and of surrender to his will, expressed in the image of the thread, is used by Catherine to express the action of divine light on the souls in purgatory, a light that purifies and raises them in the splendor of the shining radiance of God (cf. Vita mirabile, 179r).

Dear friends, in their experience of union with God Saints attain such a profound knowledge of the divine mysteries, in which love and knowledge interpenetrate, that they are of help to theologians themselves in their commitment to study, to intelligentia fidei, to an intelligentia of the mysteries of the faith, to attain a really deeper knowledge of the mysteries of faith, for example, of what purgatory is.

With her life St Catherine teaches us that the more we love God and enter into intimacy with him in prayer, the more he makes himself known to us, setting our hearts on fire with his love

In writing about purgatory, the Saint reminds us of a fundamental truth of faith that becomes for us an invitation to pray for the deceased so that they may attain the beatific vision of God in the Communion of Saints (cf. Catechism of the Catholic Church, 1032).

Moreover the humble, faithful and generous service in Pammatone Hospital that the Saint rendered throughout her life is a shining example of charity for all and an encouragement, especially for women who, with their precious work enriched by the sensitivity and attention to the poorest and neediest, make a fundamental contribution to society and to the Church.[10]

---

10   General Audience of January 12, 2010, Benedict XVI. N.p., n.d. Web.

The Treatise on Purgatory: Saint Catherine of Genoa

The writer of the Vita ends his account saying that in Catherine Heaven could be seen, a heavenly creature 'changed in everything, lost in God'; and at the same time Purgatory, a heart consumed in the fire of the love of God, in a 'martyred body' (cp. 42). In fact, Saint Catherine's teaching on Purgatory stems from a truly personal mystical experience. God made her suffer and understand the punishments of the souls that are in Purgatory with an extraordinary spiritual clarity.

The soul that goes to Purgatory is now without fault but has yet to eliminate totally the evil traces left in its being by sin. The latter, not being sufficiently erased in this life by penance, constitute the temporal punishment that must be purged, as they are the impediment that delays, that still makes impossible, union with God in Heaven.

The soul separated from the body, when it is not in the purity in which it was created, seeing itself with such an impediment, of which it cannot rid itself except through Purgatory, willingly throws itself into it. The soul that sees this, if it found an even greater Purgatory, would cast itself into it to rid itself faster of that impediment, by the impetus of the love that reconciles God and the soul.

Jesus revealed Purgatory and Hell to her. Through the Divine Fire with which she was purified in her mortal life, she was able to understand the state of the souls in Purgatory. The Lord purified her soul in the furnace of His Love (like gold, which is purified in fire from all its impurities) cleansing her from all sin of her past life, leaving her prepared to appear before Him. Jesus said to her: 'The soul is like gold, it must be purified in fire.'

God took her during her mortal life, He purified and enriched her with Divine fire, leading her to a high state of perfection, in keeping with her vocation and capacity.

She said: 'the souls in Purgatory, as I seem to understand, have no other choice than to be in that place and this is by the order of God who has done this: the souls which are in Him precisely.'

Reflecting on themselves, they cannot say: 'I committed such and such sins, I deserve to be here.' Nor can they say: 'I wish I had not committed them, as I would now be in Paradise.' Neither can they say: 'Those [souls] are leaving Purgatory before me,' or 'I will leave before [them].'

And it is because they cannot have any memory of good or evil. They have such great contentment in fulfilling God's order, and in His working in them what He wills and as He wills, that they cannot think at all of their own things.

Moreover, neither can they see their companions who are suffering there for their own sins. They are far from entertaining such thoughts; they learned the reason for the Purgatory they are suffering only once – on leaving this life. These souls, living in charity, are in the divine order, which is pure charity and they can no longer be diverted to anything, because they can no longer actually sin or merit.

The rust that sin generates is an impediment, and the fire consumes it. If something that is covered cannot correspond to the reflection of all the light of the sun – not because of a defect in the heavenly body, which continually illumines, but because of the cover that obstructs it –, once the cover is removed, the thing is laid bare to the sun.

The same happens with the rust of sin, which is as a cover of souls. In Purgatory it is consumed by fire, and the more it is consumed, the more it can receive the illumination of the true sun, which is God. And contentment grows the more the rust disappears, and the soul is laid bare to the divine ray. The one grows and the other diminishes, until the time ends. The punishment is not diminished; what diminishes is the time that one is suffering it. These souls suffer such extreme punishments that there is no language capable of describing them, and no understanding can comprehend them in the least, unless God reveals them by a special grace.

The soul itself no longer has its choice; it no longer sees except what God wants; and it does not want to see more either, but only what is ordained.

And souls, for whom those who are in the world offer alms to diminish the time of their trial, are not in a condition to turn to them with affection, but leave everything to God, who responds as He wishes. If they were able to do so, it would be a disordered attachment, which would remove them from the Divine Will, which for them would be a Hell.

If the souls in Purgatory could purify themselves by contrition alone, they would pay the totality of their debt in an instant. In fact, the impetus of their contrition is great, because of the clear light that makes them see the importance of that impediment.

So the souls in Purgatory are completely abandoned to all that God gives them, be it of joy or grief; and they can no longer turn toward themselves. And if a soul appeared before God which still had an hour to purge, it would be inflicted with great harm more cruel than Purgatory, as it would not be able to endure that supreme justice and supreme goodness. Moreover, it would be something inappropriate on God's part.

The souls in Purgatory are subject to two operations. The first is that they willingly suffer the punishments, conscious that God has had great mercy with them, given what they deserved. The other operation is the joy they experience on seeing God's order, ordained with such love and mercy towards souls. And God imprints in an instant these two visions in their minds. They, as they are in grace, can understand them according to their capacity; and this gives them a great complacency which they never lack but which is enhanced in the measure that they come closer to God.

The importance that Purgatory has is something that no human language can express, or mind understand. I see in it as much punishment as in Hell. And yet I see that the soul that felt itself so stained, would receive it as mercy, as I have already said, not considering it as anything, in a certain sense, in comparison with the stain that impedes its being united to its love. I see that the punishment of the souls in Purgatory consists more in their seeing in themselves something that displeases God, and that they have done voluntarily against God's goodness, than in whatever other punishments they could endure there. And I say this because, as they are in grace, they see the true importance of the impediment that does not allow them to approach God.

The soul was created with all the perfection of which it was capable, living according to God's order, not contaminated with any stain of sin. However, once it was infected by original sin, and then by actual sins, it lost its gifts and grace, was dead and could only be resurrected by God.

Once resurrected by Baptism, the inclination to evil remains in it, which diverts it and leads it, unless it resists, to actual sin and thus it dies again.

God resurrects it again with another special grace, but the soul remains soiled and turned in on itself, and to return to the original state in which God created it, all these divine operations are necessary, without which the soul would never be able to return to the perfection of the state in which it was created. And when the soul is in the process of regaining its original state, the inflammation of its desire to be transformed in God is such, that that is its Purgatory. It is not that it sees Purgatory as such, but that the inflamed and impeded inclination is itself its Purgatory.

This last state of love is what accomplishes this work without man, because there are so many hidden imperfections in the soul, that if man saw them, he would be plunged in despair. However, this last state of love consumes all the imperfections, and God shows it His divine operation, which enkindles in it the fire of love that consumes all the imperfections that must be eliminated.

What man judges to be perfection, for God is deficiency. In fact, all the things that man does, according to how he sees, feels, understands and desires them, including those that appear to be perfect, are full of stains. For his works to be absolutely perfect, those operations must be carried out without him; the divine operation must be in God without man.

And these operations are those that God alone does in the last operation of pure and limpid love. And for the soul these works are so penetrating and inflamed that the body, which is with it, seems to be in a rage, as if it were placed in a great fire, which never lets it be at peace, until death.

The truth is that the love of God, which redounds in the soul, as I understand it, gives it such great joy that it cannot be expressed.

However, at least for the souls that are in Purgatory, this joy does not take away from them their part of punishment. And it is that love, which is as though delayed, which causes their grief, a grief that is all the more cruel the more perfect the love of which God makes it capable. So the souls in Purgatory enjoy great contentment, but at the same time they suffer immense grief, and the one does not impede the other.

One of the great admirers of the Treatise on Purgatory was, undoubtedly, Saint Francis of Sales (1567-1622), Doctor of the Church, who had many arguments with Protestants, precisely about Purgatory. In his work published in Paris in 1639, Monsignor John Peter Camus, intimate friend of the Saint and consecrated by the latter Bishop of Belley, says:

'He reprimanded Catholic preachers who, on speaking of Purgatory, presented it only to the people from the aspect of the torments and punishments that souls suffer in it, without speaking of their perfect love for God and, consequently, of the firm contentment of which they are full given their complete union with the Will of God, a union that is so invariable, that it is not possible for them to feel the least movement of impatience or anger, or to want something other than being where they are, while it so pleases God, even if it is to the end of the age.'

PURGATORY IN THE EARLY CHURCH

The belief in Purgatory extends back to ancient times. Christians such as Tertullian, Clement of Alexandria, Origen, Cyprian and many others, believed firmly in the existence of a dwelling place where souls were purified after death. They also understood the great need for those on earth to pray for the departed.

Prior to Constantine's time as Pope, many Christians already prayed for their dead. In fact, we know that they left inscriptions on their tombs requesting prayers for their souls. On Priscilla's tomb, the inscription reads:

I beg you brothers to pray always when you come here, invoking the Father and the Son in all your prayers, that they may save Agape forever.

Nothing is said explicitly about Purgatory in the first and second centuries because, in fact, the custom was already to pray for the dead. Several inscriptions have been found in the catacombs asking for prayers for departed souls. An epitaph in seven fragments dating from the Year 370 was found in an ancient Christian cemetery in Autun, France, belonging to a man called Pectorius:

'Pectorius prays here for his mother and asks his deceased parents and brothers for a prayer. O divine race of ICHTHYS (fish), keep your soul pure among mortals, you who received the immortal source of divine waters. Temper your soul, dear friend, in the perennial waters of wisdom which distributes riches. Receive the nourishment, sweet as honey, of the Savior of the Saints; eat with avidity, having the ICHTHYS (fish) in the palms of your hands. Nourish yourself with the fish, I beg you, Lord and Savior, May my mother rest in peace, I implore you, light of the dead. Ascandius, dearest father of my soul, with my sweet mother and my brothers in the peace of the fish, remember your Pectorius.'

There are many inscriptions in the catacombs; amongst them are those mentioned below:

'Here Paphlagonien Aur. Aelianus, faithful servant of God, sleeps in peace. God, remember him in eternity.'

'O God, refresh the soul of Homullus'.

'Rolosa Antonia, may God refresh you in peace in Jesus Christ.'

'Victoria, may your Spirit be able to be refreshed in the One who is good.'

'Sylvana, may you be refreshed with the holy souls.'

'Timotea, may the eternal light illumine in Christ Jesus'.[11]

Origen

Origen was a distinguished theologian and ecclesiastical writer, who was born in Alexandria. He sees in 1 *Corinthians* 3 an allusion to Purgatory:

---

11   *Catacombs of Rome and Catholic Doctrine,* Dom Maurus Wolter, Tequi Publishers, Paris, 1872, translated from the French by Dr. Julio Lopez Morales.

'If on the foundation of Christ you have built not only gold and silver and precious stones, but also wood, cane and straw, what do you expect when the soul is separated from the body? Will you enter into Heaven with your wood and cane and straw and in this way stain the kingdom of God? Or, by reason of these obstacles you might remain without receiving a prize for your gold and silver and precious stones?

None of these cases is right. It remains therefore, for you to be subjected to fire which will burn the light materials; for our God, for those who can understand the things of Heaven, it is called the purifying fire. However, this fire does not consume the creature but what it has built, wood, cane or straw. It is manifest that the fire destroys the wood of our transgressions and then it gives back to us the prize of our great works.'

Lactantius

Lactantius was known as the Christian Cicero, mainly for his skill in the Latin language; he was born in Africa the son of pagan parents, but embraced and converted to Christianity. Like Origen, he sees in 1 *Corinthians* 3 an allusion to Purgatory:

'But when he judges the righteous, he will also test them in the fire. Then those whose sins exceed in weight and number, will be seared by the fire and burnt, but those imbued with justice and full maturity in virtue will not perceive that fire, because they have something of God in them which repels and rejects the violence of the flame.'[12]

---

12   *Purgatory, the Primitive Church, the Fathers of the Church.* By Jose Miguel Arraiz.

Felicity and Perpetua, Two Young Women Who Gave their Life for their Faith in Christ

Saint Perpetua was born in Africa and martyred on March 7, 203 in Carthage, together with Felicity, Revocatus, Saturninus, Secundus and Saturus, her catechist.

While Perpetua was in prison she had a vision of her brother Dinocrates, who died at a very early age from a cancer, which disfigured his face to the point that, Perpetua wrote, his appearance when he died horrified everyone.

In the first vision she saw Dinocrates coming out of a gloomy place with many others. He looked parched and very thirsty, with a filthy, pale appearance with the wound on his face, that he had when he died. She says: 'I trusted that my prayer for him had helped his suffering and prayed for him every day until we passed the camp of prisoners. I prayed for my brother day and night. Then, one day being prisoners, he showed me this:

I saw that the gloomy place I had seen previously was now illumined and Dinocrates had a clean body; he was well dressed, and was looking for something to refresh him, and, in place of the wound, I saw a scar. There was a pool and someone drew water from the tub incessantly, and near the edge there was a glass of water which Dinocrates took and drank. When he was satiated he left the water to play happily as children do. I then awoke and understood that he had been moved from the place of punishment.'

In the Third Century, Saint Cyprian expressed his conviction in the existence of a punishment that remains to be served after the granting of ecclesiastical peace. If the penance that preceded death was not fulfilled and the penalty not satisfied on earth, then the soul postulates an expiation after death.

At the beginning of the Third Century, in his work *De Monogamia*, Tertullian says: 'The surviving wife offers prayers for the joy of her husband in the days of the anniversary of his death, and it is understood that the wife prays for the soul of her deceased husband, so that it may soon reach the joy of Paradise.'

Saint Ephrem in His Testament

'On the thirtieth anniversary of my death remember my brothers in your prayers. The dead receive help from the prayers said by the living'. Saint Jerome attests that Saint Ephrem's writings were read in the Church after the Holy Bible'.

Saint Clement of Alexandria

Born in the Year 150, probably in Athens, Saint Clement was born of pagan parents. After he became a Christian, he traveled through Syria and Palestine and then to Alexandria were he stayed. He is considered, to be the first theological expert of Christianity. He was a man of profound knowledge, not only about Sacred Scripture but also about Christian works.

In the *Stromata,* or tapestries, he speaks about the purification by fire, that the soul suffers after death if it has not attained complete holiness.

'Through great discipline the believer strips himself of his passions and goes to the mansion that is better than the preceding one; he goes through the greatest torments taking upon himself repentance for the faults he might have committed after his Baptism. He is tortured even more on seeing that he has not obtained what others have already acquired. The greatest torments are assigned to a believer because God's justice is good and his goodness is just, and these punishments complete the course of expiation and purification' [Clement of Alexandria, *Stromata* IV, 114 (66)].

Abercius

The following paragraph, written by Abercius, was used in his epitaph:

'A citizen of a prominent city, one I built while I was living, so that I could have a place of rest for my body. My name is Abercius, a disciple of the chaste Shepherd who feeds his sheep in the mountains and fields, whose great eyes watch everything, who showed me the faithful writings on life while living. Being ready, I ordered that this be written, in my seventy-second year. May each one who understands this be in agreement with it, and may one who understands it pray'. Abercius (Abercius' Epitaph).

In the Fourth Century, the Greek Fathers affirmed the existence of Purgatory. A testimony exists describing the practice of praying for souls. In the Pauline Churches there were some apologetic practices for the deceased (1 *Corinthians* 15-29).

Before her death, Saint Monica said to Saint Augustine: 'this only I ask of you that you should remember me at the altar of the Lord.' (Taken from *Purgatory Quizzes to a Secret Preacher,* Tan Books, page 2).

Already in ancient literature the authors referred to the subject of Purgatory, as did the Italian poet, philosopher and thinker Dante Alighieri in his masterpiece *The Divine Comedy,* written around the Year 1307, which he completed shortly before his death at Ravenna in the Year 1321. In *The Divine Comedy,* which was the most important work of his time and considered one of the most significant pieces of universal literature, Dante indicates the path souls follow to attain salvation.

'Through a journey he undertakes in search of his deceased beloved, the poet passes through Hell, which he describes as nine circles which represent the darkest defects of the humanity. Heaven is a huge rose on whose petals souls dwell. He describes Purgatory as a mountain with a flat summit and slopes cut symmetrically in a series of round steps to Hell. On each step a sin is redeemed, but those who redeem them are happy because they have hope. Dante is purified of his sins because an Angel gradually erases letters of a writing that has been attached to him.

Purgatory is divided into seven cornices, where souls expiate their sins in order to be purified before entering into Paradise. As opposed to Hell, where sins become worse as one advances in the circles, in Purgatory the base of the mountain, namely the first cornice, shelters those who have the most serious offenses, whereas the less culpable sinners are at the summit closer to Eden.'

EXPERIENCE OF THE SAINTS: THOUGHTS AND REFLECTIONS ON PURGATORY

The Saints had many frightening revelations of Purgatory, indeed the Catholic Church holds vast collections of their writings which are used for the Beatification and Canonisation process. These writings describe the mystical experiences they lived through, which testify that purgatory exists.

The Italian priest Dolindo Ruotolo, a Franciscan Tertiary who is in the process of Canonization, published a book titled *Purgatory; The Last of God's Mercies*, in which he says:

'When there is talk of Purgatory, it is not unusual to present it as an inexorable and slightly less than merciless act of Divine Justice. Purgatory is certainly a place of most painful torments, in face of which the sorrows of the present life are like flowers of the field surrounded by thorns. However, although the torments of Purgatory are extremely grave, they are a loving purification to transform the soul, fitting it for the perfect happiness of Paradise.[13]

It is really a contest of love: God, who loves the soul, purifies it out of Love. The soul, which loves God, tends to Him and is happy to be purified, though suffering bitterly. This is because it ponders the gravity of its faults, which deprive the soul of the full enjoyment of union with God. It is a real contest of love between God and the soul, and it is necessary

13   *Purgatory. The Last of God's Mercies.* Ruotolo, Father Dolindo.

to eliminate from the conception of Purgatory all those false ideas which see it as the vengeance of Divine Justice, and as a terrible prison where souls languish without consolation'.

We must consider Purgatory for what it really is: 'God's last act of Mercy, which, through the necessary purification, leads the soul to the glory and happiness of Paradise.'

When the soul leaves the body, it comes out fully in the life of the Spirit: it is like a small maggot that leaves the cocoon, and goes in search of the highest good, God. Sadly, however, at that moment the soul is not as God created it, but bears within it the consequences of all its actions – actions that, at the moment it leaves the body, appear clearly before it.

'The soul in grace but partly stained, is like a pigeon with wounded wings, unable to fly, yet it tends to God with love, because of the state of grace that attracts it to Him, and seeks the way to purify itself, imploring God's Mercy. The soul in a state of grace is a traveler that has finally reached Eternal Life; however, in its purification it must continue as a traveler, until it is perfectly pure to be united at last with perfect Love.

The soul in Purgatory is saved, but needs to suffer the pains of purification because it now sees its faults, not with a human conscience but in the light of holiness.

The pains of Purgatory are a mystery to human beings, but the testimonies given directly by souls prove the pain of the punishments, which cannot be compared with the sorrows of temporal life; they are torments of the soul which it suffers incessantly.'

Saint Augustine, Saint Gregory and other Fathers say that our idea of Purgatory is far from the reality, given that the duration of these torments cannot be compared with the most terrible sicknesses or tortures of this life. When we read, in the annals of the history of the Church, accounts of the sufferings the martyrs went through for the faith and the barbarous cruelties with which they were martyred, we are horrified and yet the sufferings of Purgatory, as revealed to Saint Margaret Mary dei Pazzi, cannot be compared with these human sufferings.

In Purgatory, souls suffer directly the pain of purification, which is only attenuated by the suffrages of the living for them.

The instant the soul is separated from the body, it has perfect knowledge of its faults, offenses and sins. And, despite its love, it knows that it cannot be united to God if it has any fault. So it wants to be purified and go to Paradise without a stain. Therefore, Purgatory is a necessary and transformational state.

A Dominican religious, who was at the point of death, implored a friend of his, who was a priest to celebrate the Sacrifice of the Holy Mass for the eternal repose of his soul as soon as he died. Hardly had he expired when the priest went to the church and celebrated Mass with devotion for this intention.

When the Holy Sacrifice ended, the priest was taking off the sacred vestments, when the deceased religious appeared to him and reprimanded him severely for his hard heart and for having left him in the cruelest fire of Purgatory for a lapse of thirty years. Surprised, the priest said:

'How can it have been thirty years? It is not more than an hour since you left this life and your body does not yet show *rigor mortis.*'

The soul explained:

'Learn, my friend, the fire of Purgatory is a great torment - just one hour seems like thirty years. Learn also to have compassion for us.'

PURGATORY IN THE DIVINE PLAN

Purgatory has a very important place in our Faith since it has a leading role in the economy of man's salvation. We must consider that God's Church is made up of three parts: the Militant Church, the Triumphant Church and the Suffering Church, namely Purgatory.

The Body of Christ is quite simply the union of the three churches and therefore the three are inextricably linked. They communicate constantly, causing an alignment, which is referred to as *Communion of Saints*. The sole object of this communion is to lead souls to eternal glory; the end of all the elect.

The work of the Militant Church (the Church here on earth) is to alleviate the sufferings of departed souls. God has provided us with everything we need to release souls from the mysterious prison: simple prayers for the dead and devotion to the holy souls. It is part of our role as Catholics, and as part of the militant church, to pray and offer up sacrifices and masses for the attenuation of suffering souls. Zeal flows from the love and charity that the Holy Spirit infuses in the believers' heart.

'In the way of perfection, devotion to souls must be animated by Holy Fear and a Spirit of Faith. God is holy and no shadow of sin is tolerated in His presence.'

When iniquity is manifested in creatures, the holiness of God exacts its expiation, and when this expiation is in the midst of the rigor of justice, it is terrifying. It is because of this that Scripture says: 'Holy and venerable is His name, and the works of His hands are faithful and just' (*Psalm* 110). Because His Holiness is infinite, God's justice is perfect and He judges with extreme rigor, even the most trivial faults, as no fault can appear before Him. We must be absolutely holy to go to Heaven.

God's justice is perfect; it is perfectly just, it is exact; it does not leave anything without correction or reward. Although there is rigor in His judgment there is also mercy. And this is the reason we say that this holy devotion is infused with holy fear – a reverential fear that leads us to not want to offend God and to pray for the dead, so that those faults which aggrieved the Holy Trinity are forgiven.

It is a true act of love; God, who loves His creation, purifies man with love. The soul that loves God tends to Him, and is happy to be purified before coming into His presence. As a pure spirit, the soul has perfect knowledge that it must expiate its sins before coming to God. So, despite the pain of expiation, it knows that God awaits. Purgatory, therefore, is an act of Divine Mercy which gives the repentant soul the opportunity to be saved.

The soul in Purgatory has been saved, and is willing to suffer the pains of purification because it sees its miseries and imperfections, no longer with a human conscience, but in the light of holiness. It is conscious that it must undergo this reparation to see God and enjoy endless ineffable joy.

The pains of Purgatory are of a completely different nature from those of earthly life. The torments the soul suffers are incessant. The soul suffers directly the pain of purification, and the pain it suffers is only attenuated by suffrages and prayers, sacrifices that the living offer for the dead. This demonstrates the inextricable link between the Militant and the Purgative Church, since in gratitude, for the help of the living, souls become great intercessors for their prayers. When souls are helped with the prayer, sacrifices and good works of the living, their sufferings are attenuated. And then, when the Divine Will so disposes, they ascend to the Divine Presence and become part of the Triumphant Church. It is within our power to ensure that more souls praise and adore God in His Kingdom of love. In turn, those immensely grateful souls help us by their intercession, so that we can also participate in the Divine Glory.

'A suffrage is like the removal of a tumor which leaves the previously sick part healthy, no longer causing suffering. It is like a payment of loving charity, which removes a debt from the soul and dispenses it from paying it up to the end, relieving it from the punishments.'[14]

The torment of Purgatory is described as a burning fire, one that is very different from any earthly fire. The strongest and most searing fire of earth cannot be compared with the fire

---

14   *Purgatory*. Father Schouppe.

endured by a soul in Purgatory - a fire that is a thousand times greater in intensity than the greatest fire of earth. This is demonstrated in the life of the Polish Dominican Father Stanislaus Kostka, in the year 1590.

' While this saintly religious was praying for the souls of the dead, he saw a soul completely devoured by flames, and he asked it if the fire was more penetrating than that of earth.

"Woe is me – answered the soul screaming – compared with that of Purgatory all the fire of earth is like a soft breeze." The religious wondered: "How is it possible? I would like to feel it on the condition however, that it will serve to discount in part, the punishments I will have to suffer in Purgatory".

The soul added: "no mortal will be able to endure the least part of the fire, without dying instantly. However, if you want to be convinced, stretch out your hand."

Without hesitating, the priest stretched out his hand, on which the soul let fall a drop of its sweat or a similar liquid. The religious let out a shrill cry and fell to the ground, having fainted from the pain.

The Brothers hastened to him and gave him all the care so that he would regain consciousness. Full of terror, he told them what had happened, and he showed them a very painful wound on his hand. He was unable to stand and needed to lie down to recover, after a year and a half of incredible sufferings, he died exhorting the Brothers to flee from small faults, so as not to fall into those terrible torments.'

God allows such apparitions and manifestations for the relief of souls and for our instruction, so that we may have compassion, and understand the rigor of Divine Justice. We often regard our faults lightly, not perceiving the consequences for our soul.

Saint Margaret Mary Alacoque wrote:

'While I was praying in the presence of the Most Holy Sacrament on the feast of *Corpus Christi*, suddenly a person enveloped in fire stood before me. From the painful state in which the soul found itself, I deduced that it was in Purgatory and I wept bitterly. That soul told me he was a Benedictine who once heard my confession and ordered me to receive Holy Communion. As a reward for that, God allowed him to ask me for help while he was in torment. He asked me to offer everything I did or suffered for a period of three months. After obtaining permission from my Superior, I did what he asked. He told me that the main reason for his torments was that, in this life, he had preferred his own interests rather than God's, in a word, that he was too attached to his good reputation. The second reason was his lack of charity with his brethren. It would be difficult for me to describe what I had to endure during those three months. He never left me and a saw him as a fire suffering such terrible torments, I could do no more than groan and weep incessantly. Moved with compassion, my Superior told me to undertake harsh penances. After three months, I saw the soul shining with happiness, joy and glory. It was about to enter into eternal happiness and, on thanking me, he told me that he would protect me when he was with God' (Handwritten book on Purgatory).

Important and incredible secrets about Purgatory were revealed also to **Saint Gertrude of Helfta** as well as to **Saint Bridget of Sweden**, two Saints of great character and spirituality.

Saint Gertrude was born in Eisleben, Thuringia, in 1256. She was an orphan at the age of five and was taken into the convent of the Cistercian nuns of Helfta, Saxony by Abbess Gertrude of Hackerborn. In 1281, at 25, she had her first divine manifestation. She began to write in Latin, due to an interior impulse, and listened to Jesus' voice, who wanted her writings to be made known. Around 1284 she received the visible stigmata. Before dying at 45, she also received the gift of the Wound of the Arrow of Love in her heart. She is remembered among the initiators of devotion to the Sacred Heart.

Among her many mystical experiences, Abbess Gertrude of Hackerborn appeared to her in glory while she offered her Mass and saw that the Lord received her in His heart. In these visions, Gertrude saw the connection between the Mass, the Sacred Heart and the souls of the dead.

One day she was praying for a Brother who had died a short time before and she saw his soul with the aspect of a frog horribly burned and tormented by different punishments because of his sins. It seemed that he had something bad under his arm and an enormous weight obliged him to bend down to the ground, unable to stand straight.

Gertrude understood that he appeared bent down and in the form of a frog because during his life as a religious, he neglected to raise his mind to divine things. Moreover, she understood that the pain he had under his arm was because he had worked, with the Superior's permission, to acquire temporal goods and had hidden the earnings. He had to pay for his disobedience.

Gertrude recited the Psalms prescribed for that very soul, and she asked the Lord if it would be of some benefit: 'Certainly - Jesus answered - souls being purged come and take such suffrages, including brief prayers said with fervor, which are of great benefit to them.'

Saint Bridget of Sweden was born on June 14, 1302, daughter of Birger, governor of Uppland, which was the principal province of Sweden. Her mother, Ingeborg, was the daughter of the governor of Eastern Gotland. At the moment of Bridget's birth, the priest of Rasbo, called Benedict, was praying for the happy delivery of Lady Ingeborg. Suddenly, the priest was enveloped by a luminous cloud, in which the Most Holy Virgin appeared to him and said: 'A girl was born in Birger and her voice will be heard throughout the world.' *(Sagli die XXIV,* Aprilis 1903. *Imprimatur La Pieta).*

Her mother died young, so Bridget was educated by her pious aunt. At a very early age she felt attracted to divine things. At 10, Bridget was moved by a sermon she heard on the Lord's Passion. The following night she had a dream in which she saw the Lord nailed on the cross covered with blood and wounds. At the same time a voice said to her: 'Look at me, my daughter.' 'O my Lord,' she answered, 'who has treated you so cruelly?' Our Lord answered her: 'Those who reject me and are insensitive to my love for them.' This mysterious dream made such a profound impression on her that, from then on, she meditated continually on the sufferings of Our Lord Jesus Christ and would always weep when she did so.

At 15, out of obedience, Saint Bridget married Prince Ulf. They had eight children, including Saint Catherine of Sweden. Saint Bridget died at Rome in 1373, after returning from a pilgrimage to the Holy Land. His Holiness Saint John Paul II named her a patroness of Europe. In one of her mystical experiences she had a great revelation of the fate of souls, revelations that are recorded in the famous writings of her *Revelations*.

'Watching in prayer, the Saint saw in a spiritual vision a very great palace full of innumerable people, all in brilliant white garments, and each one apart in his seat or throne. However, there was a judicial throne higher than the others; it was occupied by One like the sun, and the light and radiance that came from Him, was incomprehensible in longitude, latitude and profundity. There was a Virgin close to the throne with a beautiful crown on her head, and all in the palace were serving the One shining like the sun, seated on the throne, offering him a thousand praises with hymns and canticles.

There appeared then I saw a Negro like an Ethiopian, terrible in aspect and bearing, as though full of envy and burning with great anger. He cried out and said: "O, just judge, render judgment on this soul for me and hear his works! Little remains of his life. Allow me to punish the body along with the soul until their separation from each other." After he had said this, it seemed to me that there stood near the seat one like a knight in arms, pure and wise in his words and modest in his bearing. He said: "O Judge, see, here are the good works that he has done up to this hour."

The voice of the sun seated on the throne was immediately heard: "There is more vice than virtue here, and it is not just that vice should be joined to the summit of virtue."

The Negro answered: "Then it is just for this soul to be joined to me, for while he has some vice in himself, there is total wickedness in me." Then the Saint saw an armed soldier next to the throne, modest in aspect, wise in words and gentle in manner, who said: "O Judge, do you see here the good works that this soul has done up to this point?"

And then a voice was heard from the throne that said: "More however, are the vices of this soul than the virtues. It is not right for vice to have a part with the highest virtue, or that it be joined to it."

The Negro said right away: "it is just that this soul be given to me; if it has vices, I am full of wickedness, and it will be all right with me."

"God's Mercy – said the soldier – accompanies everyone until death. Until the soul leaves the body, sentence cannot be passed, and this soul over which we are arguing, is still in the body and has discretion to choose the good."

"Scripture – replied the Negro – which cannot lie, says: *Thou shalt love God above all things, and thy neighbor as thyself.* And all that it has done has been out of fear, not out of love of God as it should have, and all the sins it has confessed have been with little contrition and sorrow. And as it does not merit Heaven, it is right that it be given to me for Hell as its sins are here manifested before Divine Justice, and it has never had true contrition and sorrow."

"This wretch – said the soldier – hoped and believed that, helped by grace, he would have that true contrition."

To which the Negro answered: "You have brought here all the good that it has done, all its words and thoughts that can help it to be saved; but all this does not come close to the worth of a real act of contrition and sorrow, born of divine charity with faith and hope; consequently, it cannot serve to erase its sins. Because justice is of God, determined in His eternity, that no one can be saved without contrition; and, as it is impossible for God to go against this, his eternal decree, I have good reason to ask for this soul to be tormented with eternal punishment in Hell."

"No!", replied the soldier, and then countless demons appeared, like the sparks that come out of a searing fire and in one voice they cried out, saying to the One seated on the throne who shone like the sun: "Well, we know that you are one God in three Persons, that you are without beginning and without end, and that there is no other God but you, who are true charity, in whom mercy and justice come together.

You were in Yourself from the beginning, you do not have in You anything small or changeable, everything is fulfilled in You as is appropriate to God; outside of You there is nothing, and without You there is no happiness or joy.

"We know that you are one God in three Persons without beginning or end. There is no other god than you. You are love itself along with mercy and justice. You existed in yourself from the beginning without loss or change, as is proper to God. Outside of you is nothing, and without you nothing has any joy.

Your love alone created the angels, from no other matter than Your Divine power. You acted as mercy dictated. However, when we became inflamed with inner pride, envy, and greed, Your justice-loving charity cast us together with our burning malice out of heaven into the unfathomable and shadowy abyss that is now called hell. This is what Your charity did then. Your charity even now cannot be separated from justice in your judgments, whether it is fulfilled according to mercy or according to equity. We will go even further: If the one whom You love more than anyone, I mean, if the sinless and immaculate Virgin who begot You had sinned mortally and had died without godly contrition, Your love for justice is such that her soul would never have reached heaven but would have been with us in hell. So, Judge, why do You not sentence this soul to us, so that we may punish him according to his works?"

Then the sound of a trumpet was heard, after which all fell silent, when a voice was heard: Be silent, all of you angels, souls and demons, and hear what the Mother of God has to say!" Then the Virgin herself appeared before the judgment seat, and it looked as though she were hiding some large objects beneath her mantle, she said: "You, enemies, persecute mercy and with no charity proclaim justice. Although it is true that this soul is lacking in good works, and cannot go to Heaven because of this, look what I bring under my mantle." And lifting it on both sides, one could see a small church and some religious in it and, on the other side, men and women could be seen, friends of God, all of whom cried out with one voice saying: "Lord, have mercy on him."

Then a great silence reigned and the Virgin continued: "Sacred Scripture says that he who has true faith in the world can move mountains from one place to another. What, then, cannot the cries do of all these who had faith and served God with fervent love? What can God's friends not obtain, to whom he begged they pray for him, so that he could be spared Hell and attain Heaven, and much more when by his good works he sought no other reward than heavenly goods?

By good fortune, cannot the tears and prayers of all these Blessed help this soul and lift it, so that before he dies he has true contrition with love of God? I also will join my prayers to those of all the Saints that are in Heaven, whom he honored with particular veneration.

And to you, demons, I order you on behalf of the Judge and of His power, to attend to what you will now see in His justice." And they all answered as with one voice: "We see that, as in the world tears and contrition placate God's ire, so your petitions incline Him to mercy with love."

After this, a voice was heard that came from the One seated on the brilliant throne, who said: "Because of the prayers of my friends he will have contrition before his death and he will not go to Hell but to Purgatory with those who suffer there the greatest torments; once he has purged his sins, he will receive his reward in Heaven with those who had faith and hope, but with little charity." And, on hearing this, the demons fled.

Saint Bridget then saw that a terrible and dark chasm opened, in which there was a furnace burning inside, and the fire had no fuel other than demons and living souls that were burning. In that furnace was this most afflicted soul. It had its feet fixed in the furnace, and the rest of it raised as if it were a person; and it was not in the highest or the lowest part of the furnace. It had a terrible and frightening figure. Fire seemed to come out from under the soul's feet, which rose as when water rises in a pipe, and, compressing itself violently, passed over its head, so that a searing fire ran through all its pores and veins. The ears spewed fire like a forge, which with constant blowing tormented the whole brain. The eyes were twisted and sunken, as if fixed in the back of the neck. The mouth was open and the tongue protruded from the openings of the nose and hung down to the lips. The teeth were as sharp iron nails, fixed in the palate. The arms were so long that they reached the feet. The hands were full and squeezed filth and burning fish. The skin that covered the soul was dirty and most disgusting, so cold that just to see it made one shiver, and from the matter exuded, as from an ulcer with putrid blood, such a foul smell, which cannot be compared with anything disgusting on earth.

After seeing this torment, the Saint heard a voice that came from the depth of that soul, which said five times: "Woe is me! Woe is me!," crying out with all its strength and shedding abundant tears. "Woe is me, who loved God so little for His supreme virtues and the grace He granted me! Woe is me, who did not fear, as I should have, God's justice! Woe is me, who loved the delight of my body and my sinful flesh! Woe is me, who allowed myself be drawn by the riches of the world and vanity and pride! Woe is me, because I knew you Louis and Joan!"

And then the Angel said to Saint Bridget: "I am going to explain this vision to you. The palace you saw is like Heaven. The crowd of those who were on the seats and thrones with white and shining garments are the Angels and the souls of the Saints. The sun that was on the highest throne signified Jesus Christ in His Divinity. The woman is the Virgin Mother of God. The Negro is the devil who accuses the soul, and the soldier, the Guardian Angel, who recounts the soul's good deeds.

The fiery furnace is Hell, which is burning with so much power, that if the world with all that it has were ignited it could not be compared to the vehemence of that fire. Heard in it are different voices, all against God, and they all begin and end with Woe! And the souls seem like persons, whose members extend and are tormented by the devils without a break.

Understand, also, that although the fire you saw in the furnace burns in eternal darkness, the souls that are burning in it do not all have the same punishment. Above this darkness is the greatest punishment of Purgatory that souls can suffer. And beyond this place there is another, where a lesser punishment is endured, which consists in lack of strength, of beauty, and other such things, as if someone after a serious illness was convalescing with lack of strength and all that accompanies such a state of weakness, until little by little it returns to itself.

There is another place that is higher than these two, where there is no other punishment than the desire to see and enjoy God. And, so that you will understand it better, I am going to give you the example of a bit of metal, which would burn and mix with gold in a very searing fire, until all the metal is consumed and only pure gold remains. The stronger and denser the metal, the stronger must be the fire which is needed to separate the gold and consume the metal. On seeing the gold purified and melted like water, the craftsman puts it in another place where it takes its true shape to sight and touch, then he takes it out of there and puts it in another place to give it to its owner.

The same thing happens in this spiritual purification. In the first state, placed above the darkness of Hell, is the greatest punishment endured in Purgatory, which you saw that soul suffer. Here there are what seem like poisonous bugs and ferocious animals; there is heat and cold; there is confusion and darkness coming from the punishments of Hell, and some souls have greater torment there than others, according to the greater or lesser atonement they made for their sins before they left the body.

Then God's justice takes the soul out to other places, where there is only lack of strength, where they are detained until they have relief and help either from their personal friends or from the sacrifices and constant good works of the Holy Church. The soul that receives the greatest help convalesces faster and is freed from this state.

From there the soul goes to the third place, where there is no punishment other than the desire to be in the presence of God and to enjoy the Beatific Vision. There are many others in this state for quite some time, among whom are those that, while they lived in the world, did not have a perfect desire to reach the presence of God and enjoy seeing Him."

He also noted that many die in the world who are so just and innocent that they come immediately into the presence of God and enjoy Him; and others also die, after having atoned for their sins, so that their souls suffer no punishment. But few are the ones who do not suffer the punishment of desiring God.

Souls that are in these three states, share in the prayers and good works of the Holy Church on earth, mainly the good works they did while they were alive, as well as the works offered up for them by their friends. And as sins are of many different sorts, so too are the punishments. Souls enjoy the offering and prayers from the world, just as the starving enjoy food, and the thirsty crave water.

"God bless – continued the Angel – the one in the world who helps souls with his prayers and the work of his body, for God's justice cannot lie, which says that souls are either purified after death with the punishment of Purgatory or helped with the good works of friends and of the Church, so that they come out sooner."

After this, many voices were heard from Purgatory that said: *My Lord Jesus Christ, righteous Judge, send your love to those who have authority in the world, and then we will be able to participate more than we do now, in their song, lesson and oblation.*

Above from where these cries came there was something like a house, in which many voices were heard that said: *God reward those who help us and make up for our faults!*

Dawn seemed to be breaking in the same house and a cloud appeared that did not share in the clarity of the dawn, from which a loud voice came that said: "O Lord God, give of your incomprehensible power a hundredfold to all those in the world who help us and lift us with their good works, so that we can see the light of your Divinity and enjoy your presence and divine face."

Saint Mary Magdalen de Pazzi

'An Italian Carmelite nun, who was high in virtues and who frequently fell into spiritual ecstasy. She was born in Florence in the year 1566 in the heart of a well-off family. She was baptised with the name Catherine, and was educated in Saint John's Convent in Florence. At 10 she made a vow of virginity. Her parents pressured her to marry, but she refused, being faithful to her vocation to the religious life. At 16 she entered the convent of Discalced Carmelites and received the name Mary Magdalen. From the time she received the habit until her death she experienced a series of raptures and ecstasies. She died full of merits in 1607. The year after her death, her sepulcher was opened and her body was completely uncorrupted.

In one of her ecstasies she had the most frightening experience of Purgatory. She was taken to the different states in which a soul can be after death. Walking across the various plains prepared by Divine Mercy and Justice, she understood the holiness of God and the wickedness of sin. This event occurred one night in 1607, when the Saint was in the convent garden with several nuns. She entered into ecstasy and saw Purgatory open before her. At the same time, as she later related, a voice invited her to visit all the prisons of Divine Justice, and to see how the souls are that are detained there are so deserving of compassion. At that moment, she was heard to say: "Yes, I will go," she consented to take the painful journey. From that moment, she walked for two hours around the large garden, pausing from time to time.

Every time she interrupted her walk, she contemplated attentively the sufferings that were shown to her. The nuns saw that she felt pity, she wrung her hands, her face became pale and her body arched under the weight of suffering she experienced during the terrible spectacle she was witnessed. Then she began to lament in a loud voice: "Mercy, my God, mercy! Descend O Precious Blood and release the souls from their prison! Poor souls, they suffer so cruelly, and even so, they are happy and joyful. In contrast, the prison cells of the martyrs were gardens of delights, although there were others in greater profundity. How happy I must feel not to be obliged to go down there," however to continue on her journey she did enter through such places.

She walked a few steps and then stopped, terrified and sighing profoundly, she cried: "What? Religious are also in this horrendous dwelling?! Good God! How tormented they are, O Lord!" She went from there places of less sadness. These were the prison cells of simple souls and children who had fallen into many faults out of ignorance. The Saint felt their torments were far more bearable than the previous ones. Here there was only ice and fire, and she noticed that the souls had their Guardian Angels with them. She also saw demons of horrible shapes that increased their sufferings. Going a few steps further, she saw even more unfortunate souls than the last, and then her lament was heard:

"O what dreadful demons and horrible torments! Who, O my God, are the victims of this torture? They are being pierced by sharp swords and are cut into pieces." She was told that they were souls whose conduct had been stained by hypocrisy.

Further on, she saw a great multitude of souls who were beaten and crushed under a great pressure, and she understood that they were souls who had been impatient and disobedient in their lives. While she contemplated them, her look, her sighs, her whole attitude was full of compassion and terror.

A moment later her agitation increased and she made a painful exclamation. It was the prison cell of liars that was opening before her. After considering it attentively, she said: "liars are confined to this place of closeness to Hell, and their sufferings are exceedingly great. Molten lead is poured into their mouths; I see them burning and at the same time shivering with cold."

Then she went to the prison of those souls that had sinned out of weakness and she was heard to say: "I thought I would find them among those who sin out of ignorance, but I was mistaken: you are being burnt in a more intense fire." Further on, she perceived souls that had been too attached to the goods of the world and had sinned out of avarice. "What blindness – she said – was theirs who anxiously sought perishable fortune. Those whose former riches could not satisfy them sufficiently are now in this dreadful darkness."

Seeing ambitious and proud souls, she said: "I see those who wish to shine before men; now they are condemned to live in that darkness, anchored in torments, they melt like metal in a furnace." From there she went to a place where the imprisoned souls were those stained by impurity. She saw them in such a filthy and pestilent prison cell, that the vision gave her nausea. She turned away quickly to avoid seeing such a horrible spectacle.

Then she was shown the souls whose fault was ingratitude to God. These, prey of unspeakable torments, were drowned in a lake of molten lead, for having dried up the source of mercy with their ingratitude. Finally, in the last prison cell, she saw those who had not been given to a particular vice, but who, for lack of appropriate vigilance over themselves, had committed trivial faults. She observed there that these souls had to share in the punishment of all the vices, in a moderate degree, because those faults committed only once made them less culpable than those committed out of habit.

After this station, the Saint left the garden, begging God that she might never again have to witness such a horrible spectacle: she felt that she would not have the strength to endure it.' Pope Benedict XVI described Saint Mary Magdalen dei Pazzi as an 'an emblematic figure of a living love that refers to the essential mystical dimension of every Christian life'.

A View of Purgatory

The episode we will now recount occurred on November 17, 1859, in the convent of the Franciscan Tertiaries of Foligno, Italy.

'Almost two weeks earlier, the teacher of the novices, Sister Teresa Gesta, had died from a vascular cerebral accident. Her successor, Sister Ana Felicia, heard strange groans that day coming from the clothes closet that the deceased usually looked after. Her fear notwithstanding, Sister Anna went to the closet where she heard Sister Teresa's voice, complaining of pain and suffering. Though astonished, Sister Ana was able to ask her the reason for her complaint, to which the deceased answered, that the cause was the freedom given to the novices in regard to the vow of poverty. Then, the place filled with smoke and the silhouette of Sister Teresa appeared and went to the door and exclaimed: "Behold a testimony of God's Mercy!"

Immediately, the shadow touched the upper plank of the door and left her right hand carved in the wood burning it until she finally disappeared. A terrified Sister Ana began to shout in search of help, when the rest of the Sisters responded to her call and heard the story they saw the mark imprinted on the door. The community of the convent began to pray, to go to Communion and to do penance for the soul of the deceased. They were tempted to remove the mark that caused such horror throughout Foligno. Sister Teresa appeared again to Sister Ana to reprimand her: "Do you want to erase the sign I left printed? It is not up to you to do so, this prodigy is ordained by God for the teaching and emendation of all. Because of His Just and tremendous judgment, I have been condemned to suffer the terrible flames of Purgatory for forty years, because of the weaknesses I had with some of our Sisters. I thank you and your companions for your many prayers, which in his goodness the Lord has deigned to apply exclusively to my poor soul."

It must have been the next day when, at night, Sister Teresa communicated with her again to say joyfully that she was going to glory thanks to the prayers and penances of those who had been her companions. The image was transformed into a light white cloud, which flew to Heaven and disappeared.' In the presence of many witnesses, once the final investigation had begun, Sister Teresa's body was exhumed, and the burnt mark on the door was found to exactly correspond with that of the hand of the dead nun. The mark is still kept with veneration in the convent.[15]

Report of Father Berlioux

He describes the benefits that souls receive from persons who pray and do penance for those in Purgatory on earth. Help that is obtained primarily at the moment of death, in which we will all be strongly tempted by the devil. That is why in the *Hail Mary* we say 'pray for us now and at the hour of our death.' He tells the story of a woman who consecrated her whole life to help souls.

' The hour of her death having arrived, she was assaulted furiously by the devil who saw her about to escape from him. It seemed like the whole abyss surrounded her with all its infer-

---

15   Digital Review *Fides et Ratio*

nal cohorts. The dying woman struggled for a long time with painful efforts, when she saw a multitude of unknown persons enter her house, radiant with beauty, who put the devil to flight and, approaching her, expressed heavenly words of encouragement and consolation. Sighing she said: "Who are you?" The good visitors answered: "we are the dwellers of Heaven that your help put on the path to happiness and, in gratitude, we have come to help you to cross the threshold of eternity and to free you from the place of anguish and introduce you into the joy of the Holy City."

With these words, a smile illumined the dying woman's face, her eyes closed and she fell asleep in the peace of the Lord. Her soul found so many protectors and advocates in the souls she had liberated that, acknowledged worthy of glory, she entered Heaven triumphantly with those she had freed from Purgatory.'

Saint John Mary Vianney – The Holy Cure of Ars

He was born in Dardilly, France, on the outskirts of Lyon, on May 8, 1786. He was a diocesan priest of the Third Order of Saint Francis, who had to surmount innumerable difficulties to become a priest. His zeal for souls, his catechesis and ministry in the confessional transformed the town of Ars, which became a place of pilgrimage where crowds went in search of the holy parish priest. He prayed for long hours before the Most Blessed Sacrament and spent 16 to 18 hours a day in the confessional, working wonders in the souls of penitent faithful. He died at Ars in 1859.

Given his great spiritual virtues, this great Saint and patron of priests, reached the honor of the altar. In one of his beautiful sermons he spoke to his community about the expiation of sins after death and where souls go at the moment they leave this earthly world.

This is what he said about Purgatory in his sermon:

'I come to remind you again of the goodness and all the love you were given when you were in this world. And I come to tell you that many of them are suffering in Purgatory, they weep and beg urgently for the help of your prayers and your good works. I seem to hear them cry out in the depth of the fires that devour them: "Tell our loved ones, our children, all our relatives how huge are the demons that are making us suffer. We throw ourselves at your feet to implore the help of your prayers. Oh, tell them that since we were separated, we have been burning amidst flames! Who can remain indifferent in face of the suffering that we are enduring?"

Do you see, dear children? Do you listen to this tender mother, to that dedicated father, to all those relatives who have looked after you and helped you?

My friends, they cry out —"free us from these punishments," you can do so. Consider then, my dear brothers: a) The magnitude of the sufferings that the souls in Purgatory endure; b) the means you have to mitigate them: your prayers, and above all the Holy Sacrifice of the Mass, and do not doubt the existence of Purgatory -- it would be a waste of time.

Let no one among you have the least doubt. The Church, to whom Jesus Christ promised the guidance of the Holy Spirit, cannot, consequently, be mistaken and mislead. She teaches us about Purgatory in a positive and clear way and it is, certainly, the place where the souls of the just complete the expiation of their sins before being admitted to the glory of Paradise, which is assured to them.

Yes, my dear brothers, it is an article of faith: if we do not do penance in proportion to our sins even when we are forgiven in the Sacred Tribunal, we will be obliged to expiate them [...] In the Sacred Scriptures there are many texts that point out that even when our sins are forgiven, the Lord imposes the obligation to suffer difficulties in this world or the flames of Purgatory in the next.

See what happened to Adam. Because of his repentance, God forgave him; nevertheless, He condemned him to do penance for nine hundred years, something which is beyond what one can imagine. And I also see David who, going against God's will, ordered the census of his subjects, but later, suffering pangs of conscience, saw his own sin, and throwing himself on the ground, begged the Lord to forgive him. Moved by his repentance, God, in fact, forgave him. However, despite this, he told him that he would have to choose between three punishments that He prepared for him given his iniquity: a plague, war or famine. And David said: "I prefer to fall into the Lord's hands (given that His graces are many) than into the hands of men." And he chose the plague that lasted three days, and took seventy thousand of his subjects. If the Lord had not held back the hand of the Angel, which was extended over the whole city, Jerusalem would also have been laid waste. Considering the many evils caused by his sins, David begged God for the grace to punish him alone and not the people, who were innocent.

How many years, my dear children, will we have to suffer in Purgatory who have so many sins, and who, with the pretext of having gone to confession, do not do penance or shed a single tear? How many years of suffering must we expect for the next life in Heaven? When the Holy Fathers tell us of the torments they suffer in such a place they seem like the sufferings endured by Our Lord Jesus Christ in His Passion.

The fire of Purgatory is the same as that of Hell, except that it is not forever. If a soul came surrounded by fire and appeared here before you with its cries and sobs it would end up by softening your hearts.

The souls would say: "O how we suffer, take us out of these torments, you can do so!"

Yes, dear brothers, people judge very differently in the flames of Purgatory about venial sins, if it is that one can call slight the sins that lead to endure such rigorous punishments. **Saint Teresa** said:

"My God, what soul will be sufficiently pure to be able to enter into Heaven without passing through the purifying flames? In her last illness she suddenly cried out: "O justice and power of my God, how terrible they are!" During her agony God allowed her to see His Holiness as the Angels and the Saints see it in Heaven; it so terrified her that, seeing her shake very agitated, her Sisters said weeping: "O Mother, what is happening to you?" "I do not fear death; I desire only to be united forever to my God. I fear for my sins and for something more; I tremble for the account it is necessary to render God, who at that moment will not be merciful."

The Sisters were very perturbed and they asked: "Is it Hell?" She said: "No, that, thank God, is not for me. O my Sisters, it is the Holiness of God. My life must be placed face to face with that of the Lord Jesus Christ himself. Woe is me if I have the slightest stain. Woe is me if there is a shadow of sin!"

How will our deaths be, brothers, if in our penance and good actions we have never purged a single sin in the tribunal of penance? How many years and centuries of punishment we would have. God is just in everything and He rewards the slightest action; He gives us fully what we might desire. A good thought, a good desire, in other words, the desire to do some good work even when we are not able to achieve it.

He never leaves us without a reward, but also if it is a question of punishing us, He does so with rigor, even for slight faults, for which we will be sent to Purgatory. Many Saints did not go directly to Heaven. They had to pass first through the flames of Purgatory.

Saint Damian recounted how his sister had to spend several years in Purgatory for having listened to a malicious song with some approval. It is said that two men religious promised one another that the first one to die would tell the other about the state he was in. God allowed one to die first and to appear to his friend.

He told him that he had stayed in Purgatory for 15 years for having spent much time doing things his own way, and when his friend congratulated him for having stayed there such a short time, the deceased replied: "I would have preferred to be flayed alive for ten thousand consecutive years instead of the suffering of the flames." A priest told one of his friends that God had condemned him to Purgatory for several months for having delayed in the execution of a project of good works.

Albert the Great, a man whose virtues shined so greatly, said about this matter that one day he revealed to a friend that God had taken him to Purgatory for having been conceited about his own knowledge. What is astonishing is that there were Saints there, even those who were beatified, suffering their passage through Purgatory.

Saint Severino, Archbishop of Cologne, appeared to a friend a long time after his death and told him that he was in Purgatory for having postponed, until nighttime, the prayers he should have said in the morning. "O how many years of Purgatory there will be for those Christians that have not the least difficulty in deferring their prayers to the following day, with the excuse of having more urgent work! If we really want the happiness of having God we must avoid both small faults as well as great ones, as separation from God is a torment for all souls."[16]

Saint Stanislaus

When he was Bishop of Krakow, Saint Stanislaus purchased an item for the Church from a citizen called Peter Miles. In good faith, both the Bishop and Don Peter agreed to the stipulated price without any formal proof or receipt of payment.

Three years after Don Peter's death, one of his heirs decided to raise an appeal to King Boleslav requesting that the Bishop

16   www.apologeticasiloe.com

return the object to the family. The heirs of Don Peter knew that the King did not have a good opinion of the Holy Bishop, given that the latter, in fulfillment of his duties, exhorted him publicly and warned him about his evil ways. And so they knew the King would welcome the lawsuit against the Holy Bishop. The lawsuit alleged that the possession acquired by the Holy Bishop, was obtained illegally and was therefore the property of Don Peter's heirs. Since there was no proof that this was false they were certain of the Saint's defeat.

The Bishop was obliged to restore the property and make his defense in public. The Bishop claimed that if the living did not give witness of the truth, he would look among the dead for one to testify. He asked for a three-day period to present the seller, Don Peter Miles to the court.

The Saint, assured that the deceased would appear before justice made his request. It was received with laughter, but it was granted, as it was an opportunity to ridicule him. The Saint left the court and, gathering his priests, prayed and fasted for three days. On the third day, the Saint celebrated Mass and once the ceremony ended, the people and the clergy went in procession to the cemetery, where three years before Don Peter had been buried. The Bishop ordered that the stone be lifted, and that the body be taken out of the earth.

When the skeleton of the deceased appeared, the Saint knelt down, raised his eyes to Heaven and prayed for the reanimation of the deceased. He touched the bones with his pastoral staff and he said: "Peter, listen to the voice of the Lord. In the name of the Father, of the Son and of the Holy Spirit, I order you to get up and come with me to give witness of the truth".

Immediately the bones came together and were covered with flesh in the sight of all. The dead man came out of his tomb before the whole town; the living dead man went to the court and said: "I received the right price for the possession from the holy prelate, the contract was legal, my heirs are not right in their pretension. If you do not desist from your decision to bother the right possessor, I warn you that soon, after an unhappy death you will have to appear before the tribunal of the incorruptible Judge to give an account of your iniquitous pretension."

On hearing this, the King had no option but to exact justice and return the possession to Saint Stanislaus's church. Stanislaus asked Peter if he wanted to return to earth for a time, but the latter answered that would prefer to die again, returning to the sepulcher rather than run the risk of sinning.

He was still in Purgatory suffering atrocious torment, but he preferred to return because he was sure of his salvation. He would be foolish to involve himself in the world again where he may run the greater danger of being condemned. "The only grace I ask you is that you implore God's Mercy for me, so that I will come to the end of my sufferings soon, help me with your suffrages."

Arriving at the sepulcher again, Peter entered it; the Bishop ordered that the commendation of the soul be read out, during which, in one and the same instant the man was seen, and then only the bones remained where they were before, thus dying for a second time to eternal life.

In one of the apparitions of the Most Holy Virgin Mary at Fatima, she revealed to Sister Lucia – one of the young visionaries –, that a friend of hers called Amelia, who was between 18 and 20 years old, would be in Purgatory until the end of the world.[17] The works and experiences that the Church has gathered about souls in Purgatory are so innumerable that it would be impossible to compile them in a single text.

A very interesting work of our times entitled *Read Me or Rue It*, describes in an incredible way how the souls have such enormous gratitude for those who pray for them and help to alleviate their sufferings.

Saint Catherine of Bologna said:

"I have received many favors from the Saints, but much greater ones from the holy souls in Purgatory."

When they are finally freed from their punishments and enjoy the blessedness of Heaven, they never forget their friends on earth; their gratitude is boundless. Prostrate before God's throne, they pray constantly for those who helped them and they pray that they will see their benefactors in Heaven. With their prayers they protect their friends, they help them, and protect them from the demons that assail them.

---

17   Taken from *Great Promises of the Virgin*. Jeremias Lopez. Page 150, Libreria Espiritual. *The Future of Spain in the Fatima Documents*. Antonio Maria Martins, SJ, page 132. Catholic Editions Publisher. C/ Maldonado, 1.280006. Madrid

Saint John Massias, a Dominican priest, had great devotion to the souls in Purgatory. By his prayers, especially the recitation of the Holy Rosary, he obtained the release of 1,400,000 souls.

As a reward he obtained for himself the most abundant and extraordinary graces and those souls came to console him on his deathbed. Indeed this description of the event was inserted in the Bull that decreed his beatification.

Cardinal Baroni recalls a similar event. He was called to help a dying man. While he was beside the man, an army of blessed spirits suddenly appeared around his deathbed. They consoled the dying man and dispelled the demons who groaned in a desperate attempt to see his ruin. When the Cardinal asked them who they were, they answered that they were the 8,000 souls that this man had freed from Purgatory thanks to his prayers and good works; they were sent by God to take him to Heaven without spending any time in Purgatory.

Saint Vincent Ferrer prayed for his sister after she died and offered several Masses for her release. She appeared to him and said that were it not for his intercession, she would have remained for a long period of time in Purgatory.[18]

---

18   *Read Me or Rue It* EDM. Engant de Marie, initials with which Father O. Sullivan identifies himself (www. Scribd.com/doc/48541181Libro-Almas-del-Purgatorio).

Saint Pio of Pietrelcina

Narrated in the work *The Poor Souls: A Padre Pio Reminder,* by Reverend Father Paul O. Sullivan, O.P., are some of the wonderful experiences that Padre Pio had with the holy souls in Purgatory.

'This statement of Padre Pio left his monastery companions astounded. Padre Pio was visited by masses of people, but he highlighted the fact that his contact with the souls in Purgatory exceeded that which he had with the living. From the testimonies of Padre Pio's spiritual children and the events reported in the friars' chronicles, it is obvious that the association with this supernatural experience is not fantasy but a real event. He saw these souls, not with his spiritual eyes, but physically and in the reality of his earthly surrounding.

One day Padre Pio was dining with his friars in the refectory when, suddenly, he stood up and went to the monastery entrance door and engaged in a conversation with people who were not visible to the friars. But on seeing the Saint approach the door, they followed him. They heard Padre Pio speaking to someone they could not see, the friars said to one another, "he's gone mad". Finally they asked Padre Pio to whom was he speaking. With a smile, he answered: "O, don't worry, I was talking with some souls who, on their way from Purgatory to Heaven, stopped here to thank me because I remembered them in this morning's Mass. Having said this, he returned to the refectory as if nothing extraordinary had happened."

Another significant interaction with souls occurred during the Second World War. One evening after supper, when the monastery doors were closed, the friars heard some voices coming from under the stairs of the entrance and heard: "Hail, Padre Pio." The Superior, Father Raffaele, called the porter, Brother Gerard and told him to go to the first floor and ask the people there to leave, as he had not given permission for them to enter.

Brother Gerard obeyed; the corridor was totally dark and deserted and he found the door firmly locked with two steel catches. He reported this to the Superior, who the following day asked Padre Pio for an explanation of what had happened. Padre Pio explained to the Superior that the voices which were shouting "Hail Padre Pio" were those of soldiers who fell in the war, who came to thank him for his prayers.

Padre Pio burned with love for Jesus; he felt a great tenderness and pity for souls in Purgatory. During a week of discussions with seminarians, Padre Pio spoke to them about the great sufferings of the souls in Purgatory and our duty to help them with prayer, mortification and the offering of our work to gain merits for them.

Padre Pio said: "The Most Holy Virgin Mary wants us to help the souls in Purgatory. No mother loves her dying children with so much tenderness and love as the Virgin Mary. She hastens to help them in Purgatory, and is desperate to have them with her in Heaven. We give her great joy every time we help a soul to come out of Purgatory. It is impossible to know the intense gratitude of souls for those who help them. They respond with an immense desire to return the favors received. They pray for their benefactors with constant and intense fervor."

For Lack of Diligence

One afternoon, while the friars were having supper in the dining room (this happened between the years 1921 - 1922), Padre Pio was praying in the choir loft.

During that time he did not go to the dining room for supper, instead he would stay in the choir loft, and join the friars later to warm himself near the communal fireplace. Suddenly, he heard a scratching noise coming from the church, on the side of the altars.

He strained his ear to be sure that he was not imagining things. Suddenly, there was another noise: the sound of candles and candelabra falling from the upper part of the main altar, breaking the silence of the church.

At first, Padre Pio thought it must be one of the students who had had knocked the candles during the course of his daily work. He walked over to the balcony of the choir, to see more closely. He was surprised to see a motionless young friar beside the altar. "What are you doing there?" asked Padre Pio with authority. He did not get an answer. He continued: "This is a nice way to do your job! Instead of putting things in order, you break the candles and candelabra!"

However, the friar's silence was sepulchral and he continued motionless. Then Padre Pio said in a louder, more authoritative voice: "What are you doing there at this hour?"

The small friar then answered: "I am spending my Purgatory here. I was a student in this monastery and now I must amend for the errors I committed during my time here, mainly for my lack of diligence in my work at this church."

Padre Pio said to him: "Okay, listen. I will say the Mass for you tomorrow, but you must not come back here again."

With his heart beating unusually fast, Padre Pio left the choir and went to the communal fireplace, where he met his brothers. They immediately noticed his agitation and they asked him the reason: but he avoided their inquisitive eyes and only said that he felt very cold. Less than ten minutes passed when Padre Pio asked one of the friars if he would accompany him to the church. They found candles and candelabra overturned. Padre Pio wanted to be sure that he had heard correctly and that his imagination was not playing tricks on him.

Later, when he spoke of what had happened, he concluded with this observation: "for of lack of diligence in fulfilling his duty, that friar was still in Purgatory, sixty years after his death! Imagine, then, how long and how difficult Purgatory will be for those who commit much more serious sins."[19]

If we consider the number of souls that regularly visited Padre Pio it is clear that many of those souls were suffering and were desperate for prayers. Indeed there are many people who asked him about the state and position of their deceased friends and dear ones. Padre Pio always gave a direct answer, as we shall see now. This is the story of Nina Campanile:

---

19   *Voce di Padre Pio,* vol. 11, No. 5 (1978): 15.

'At the beginning of September 1916, Padre Pio arrived at San Giovanni Rotondo, and immediately many people exclaimed around the village "a holy friar has arrived"

At that time a very sad event had shaken our family. Our brother Pasqualino died in a battle on the sixteenth of that very month. One day my mother, who was worried about her son's fate, said to me: "go and ask Padre Pio if your brother has saved his soul."

I stubbornly refused: "Saints are in Heaven, not on earth." But my mother insisted more persistantly, so I asked my teacher, Vittorina Ventrella to accompany me, to see the friar. I saw Padre Pio on October 5, and Miss Ventrella introduced me and explained the reason for my visit. Father looked at me severely and said: "If the Mercy of God was as you think it should be, the whole of humanity would be in Hell. Yes, he has been saved and he needs prayers."

Meanwhile I became a spiritual daughter of Padre Pio and I began to frequent the friar regularly, but I never mentioned my brother again. On Christmas Eve of 1918, I decided to break my silence. While we were waiting for midnight in the sacristy, I said: "Father, where is my brother now?" He answered: "He is up there (in Paradise)." You can imagine the happiness I felt.'[20]

---

20   IASANZANIRO M. (PADRE), ms. 1-2.

Saint Faustina Kowalska
Secretary of Divine Mercy

Saint Faustina was born in Poland in the village of Glogowiec, at present the province of Konin. She was baptised Elena, but when she received the habit she took the name Faustina. Our Lord Jesus Christ appeared to Saint Faustina giving her the mission to propagate his Divine Mercy to the whole world, for the salvation and remedy of all souls, especially for all sinners. Heaven, Hell and also Purgatory were revealed to Saint Faustina, an event narrated in her Diary *Divine Mercy in My Soul*:

'Shortly after, I fell ill [20]. The dear Mother Superior sent me with two other sisters for a rest to [21] to Skolimow, not far from Warsaw. It was at that time that I asked the Lord who else I should pray for. Jesus said that on the following night He would let me know for whom I should pray.

[The next night] I saw my Guardian Angel, who told me to follow him. In an instant, I was in a misty place full of fire in which there was a great crowd of suffering souls. They were praying fervently, but to no avail for themselves; only we can come to their aid. The flames which were burning them did not touch me at all. My Guardian Angel did not leave me for an instant. I asked these souls what their greatest suffering was. They answered me in one voice that their greatest torment was longing for God. I saw Our Lady visiting the souls in Purgatory. The souls call her "The Star of the Sea." She brings them relief.

I wanted to talk with them some more, but my Guardian Angel beckoned me to leave. We went out of that prison of suffering. [I heard an interior voice] which said: **"My Mercy does not want this, but justice demands it."** Since that time, I am in closer communion with the suffering souls.

36. (14) Once I was summoned to the judgment [seat] of God. I stood alone before the Lord. Jesus appeared such as we know him during His Passion. After a moment, his wounds disappeared except for five: those in His hands, his feet and his side.

Suddenly I saw the complete condition of my soul as God sees it. I could clearly see all that is displeasing to God. I did not know that even the smallest transgressions will have to be accounted for.

What a moment! Who can describe it? - To stand before the thrice Holy God! Jesus asked me, "Who are you?" I answered, "I am your servant, Lord."

"You are guilty of one day in Purgatory." I wanted to throw myself immediately into the flames of Purgatory, but Jesus stopped me and said, 'What do you prefer, to suffer now for one day or for a short while on earth?"

I answered: "Jesus, I want to suffer in Purgatory, and I want to suffer also the greatest pains on earth, even if it were until the end of the world." Jesus said:

"One [of the two] is enough; You will go back to earth, and there you will suffer much, but not for long; you will accomplish My will and My desires, and a faithful servant of Mine will help you to do this, Now rest your head on My bosom, on My heart, and draw from it strength and power for these sufferings, because you will find neither relief nor help nor comfort anywhere else. Know that you have much, much to suffer, but don't let this frighten you; I am with you."

594. One evening, one of the deceased Sisters, who had visited me a few times, appeared to me. The first time I had seen her, she had been in great suffering, and then gradually these sufferings had diminished; this time she was radiant with happiness, and she told me she was already in heaven.

She told me that God has tried (58) our House with tribulation because the Mother General had doubted, not believing what I said about this soul. And further, as a sign that only now was [she] in heaven, God would bless our House.

Then she came closer to me, embraced me sincerely and said: "I must go now." I understood how closely the stages of a soul's life are bound together; that is to say, life on earth is purgatory and in heaven [the Communion of Saints].

1375. (24) After Vespers today, there was a procession to the cemetery. I could not go because I was on duty at the gate. But that did not stop me from praying for the dear souls. As the procession was returning from the cemetery to the chapel, my soul felt the presence of many souls. I understood the great justice of God, how each one must pay off the debt to the last cent.'

Blessed Anne Catherine Emmerick and Her Visions of Purgatory

Anne Catherine was born on September 8, 1774 in the village of Flamske, three kilometers from Koesfield, Germany. From the age of four she had frequent visions of the history of salvation. She received the stigmata which caused her enormous sufferings and she lived the Passion of Our Lord Jesus Christ.

In addition to the stigmata, God granted her many mystical gifts, among them: visions, locutions and ecstasy. In her last years she was nourished only on the Holy Eucharist. Given her heroic virtues, she was declared Venerable at the end of the Nineteenth Century. She was beatified by Saint John Paul II on October 3, 2004.

This great mystic made incredible visits to Purgatory, some of which we now describe:

'I see in general many souls held on earth to be saints who are still in Purgatory and, therefore, they do not enjoy the Beatific Vision. However, in this vision I saw Purgatory as the Purging Church and I saw a dark vast vault where souls seemed to be already free of their passion. There was the red light of a candle on a sort of altar and I saw an Angel come, to console the souls with a present. This happens a few times a year, but as the Angel disappeared, with him disappeared all everything that was ecclesiastical. I also understood that the poor souls, who can do nothing for themselves, pray for the Church.

When I see a general picture of the Church, I always see between the West and the North a dark and profound lake, where there is not a single ray of sun, and I think that Hell is there.

O, if men saw this clearly as I see it, all would work in this garden with more diligence than I, myself, do! When I enter a cemetery and these objects are represented to me, I can make a judgment on the zeal and charity of a nation, just as one can appreciate the diligence and laboriousness of its inhabitants, only by seeing the fields and kitchen gardens in it. Many times God has given me the grace to see many souls of Purgatory go up to Heaven with infinite joy.

However, there is no work or help in necessity without combat, effort and struggle. This happened to me. As a very young girl and as a strong maiden, I was often disturbed, frightened and mistreated in my prayer in cemeteries by evil spirits and even by the devil. I was surrounded by terrible noises and apparitions; I was frequently thrown down on the sepulchers and severely shaken. Sometimes they wished to take me out of the cemetery violently.

However, with God's grace I was never intimidated nor did I yield an inch to the enemy; instead, I redoubled my prayer, where I was most disturbed. How many graces I have received from the blessed souls of Purgatory! I wish that everyone would participate with me in this joy of helping souls! What an abundance of graces there are on earth! Yet how many souls are forgotten and graces wasted, while holy souls sigh for them!

These souls are there, in different places, suffering different torments. They are anguished and longing to be helped and saved. Yet, no matter how great their affliction and need, they praise Our Lord and Savior. All that we do for them gives them infinite joy.'

She saw in Purgatory souls in different conditions.

All Souls Day, November 2, 1819.

'I arrived with my guide at a dark place, where there were many souls. Having penetrated that place, I consoled them. Those souls were immersed in darkness, some up to their neck, others up to their waist. There were some together with others, but each one in its own prison.

Some suffered thirst; others cold; others heat; they could not help themselves. They suffered unspeakable torments and felt great longing to come out of there.

I saw that many obtained their freedom; their joy was unimaginable. Rising to a higher place in great number, in a grey spiritual way; they received during this brief transit the garments and insignias proper to the state of each, mirroring their earthly life. The place where they gathered was of ample space, above Purgatory, fenced in as a barrier of thorns.

I saw there many freed doctors, who were received by a procession of other doctors and led above. I also saw that many soldiers were released, and the happiness of these unfortunate ones destroyed in war delighted my heart. I saw few nuns and even fewer judges, but I did see many maidens, who would have consecrated themselves to God in the religious state had the circumstances been propitious, sought and gathered by other blessed women religious.

I saw some former kings and souls belonging to royal families, quite a few priests and many peasants. I saw the souls of many persons known to me and others of foreign countries, judging from their clothes. Each one of the various social states was raised in different directions by souls of the same state. While this elevation lasted, they lost their earthly insignias and received a brilliant garment of glory.

In Purgatory not only did I know my friends, but also my relatives, whom I had never seen. Among the most abandoned souls I saw were those poor ones that no one remembers and whose number is great, because many of our brothers in the faith do not pray for them. I always pray for these poor forgotten souls.'

'Tonight I was in Purgatory. It seemed to me I was led to a deep abyss. There was a great space there. It is pitiful to see how sad poor souls are in that state. However, on their face there is something that reveals the joy of their hearts when they consider the Lord's Mercy. I also saw the Mother of God on a magnificent throne; she was more beautiful than anyone I had ever seen.

Tell the faithful in the confessional (Anne Catherine was addressing Dean Rensing who was present), to pray fervently for the souls in Purgatory, because they, being very grateful, will certainly pray much for their benefactors. Prayer for souls is very pleasing to God, as by this means the enjoyment of His presence is anticipated for them.

Most of the men who are there are expiating the indifference with which they ordinarily regarded venial sins. This prevents them from practicing acts of kindness, meekness and from obtaining victories over themselves. The relation of the souls in Purgatory with earth is so delicate that just by desiring their good and alleviating and consoling them from earth, they receive great consolation. How much good one does who is constantly denies himself in favor of them, wishing intensely to help them!

From there I kept walking North. I cannot figure out exactly in what region Purgatory is. Most of the time I walk towards the North, but I lose my way and have to pass through dark places, surmounting many difficulties and obstacles, and I must suffer toils, such as those posed by water, snow, brushwood and swamps. I surmount them all out of love for souls.

Afterwards as if I descended frequently by a dark and unsteady path, under the earth, I then enter into more or less somber, nebulous, cold places, altogether inhospitable, and passing from one place to another up to souls that are in high or profound places, in places that are regularly accessible.

Tonight I have gone from one point to another. I have consoled souls and I have received from them the charge to do different works, such as praying the Litany of the Saints and the seven penitential Psalms. My guide told me that I should try not to get angry, but rather to offer all the adversities that happened to me for the holy souls. By morning I no longer remembered this piece of advice. I was just about to get angry, but I was able to control myself and I was happy about this and thanked my Guardian Angel who helped me. It is not possible to tell the great consolation that souls obtain through some small sacrifice or triumph over ourselves.

There is a soul that will remain in Purgatory until the end of the world' (July 13, 1821).

Vision after contemplating the life and martyrdom of Saint Margaret.

'Then I saw a dreadful picture. At first I did not know how it related to this Saint. I saw a large and dreadful wild boar that appeared from a deep and stinking place. I was shaking and alarmed. It was the soul of a Lady of Paris. She told me that I could not pray for her, because there was no possibility for me to help her as she had to stay and wallow in that filth until the end of the world, but that I should pray for her daughter, so that she would be converted and not be the cause of the many evils and misfortunes her mother had occasioned.

I had a vision of Saint Margaret inside a small Paris chapel, the only section remaining of a former abbey. Kept there is a part of the Saint's arm and her skull. After I venerated those bones, I saw that lady's soul and a picture of her life. Her tomb is not far from this chapel. She was of very high rank and was the cause of grave evils during the Revolution.

Because of her, many priests lost their life. However, in the midst of her vicious habits she had had from her childhood a certain veneration for Saint Margaret, and she was able to prevent the Saint's chapel from being destroyed.

Because of this, with the intercession of the Saint, she obtained the grace to be able to implore the help of prayers for her daughter, to impede the continuation and consequences of her own sins. I saw her daughter in a high and distinguished social position, engaging with the worst and most dangerous parties of that country.

All sorts of deceased persons, whom I had known a long time ago, came asking me for help. They led me around dark and narrow pools and places, where they have to do all kinds of toil, which they are never able to finish, because something – a tool or instrument – is always lacking. All begged for my help, and with toil and great effort I had to do this or that job for them, which gave them relief. Most of the jobs were rural. Between jobs I would return home and then I had to start a new job. I did much work as a vine-grower for some priests, and in a place where there were many pointed sticks where people could not move without being hurt. I fell in that place and was hurt with one of those sticks in the fleshy part of my leg and bled a lot.

For several days, as the Solemnity of the Dead approached, Anne Catherine had much work to do during the night and frequent dealings with known and unknown souls. Souls and her Guardian Angel are the ones who entrust her with different expiations, jobs or visits to relatives to do reparation for goods unjustly kept.

A woman appeared repeatedly to her asking her to persuade her daughter to restore some unjustly acquired goods from her ancestors, which she had given to her daughter. Anne Catherine had to reprove her, undertaking a long journey through the snow of the high mountains and she remembered a spiritual Church in which she had to help at the Mass, administering the Sacrament to some souls. I felt great fear, although I handled everything using small cloths. I felt I could not touch them since I am a woman.

To serve in the Mass also caused me much anguish, until the priest turned to me and ordered me to do so in a serious manner, saying that it was God's will. I recognised in that priest the good soul, now luminous and brilliant, of Abbot Lambert. I do not have clearer ideas of this scene, and I do not understand it.

Tonight I invoked with great determination the Saints whose bones I have here with me. I have invited especially my blessed sisters Magdalen of Hadamar, Columba of Bamberg, Juliana of Luttith and Liduvina to come with me to Purgatory to take the souls most loved by Jesus and Mary out of there. I had the joy of seeing many of those souls helped and freed.

The holy souls are instructed by Angels of how they may come closer to attaining salvation. This is what happened with the soul of a youth who begged me to pray for his mother. These souls can do absolutely nothing to help themselves. There is no nature in Purgatory, no trees or fruits. Everything is colorless, clear or dark, according to the degree of the souls' purification. The places where souls are have a certain order.

Judgment is passed on souls; I see it instantly in the very place in which men die. I see there Jesus, Mary, the Holy Patron of each one of them and their Guardian Angels. I see Mary Most Holy even in the judgment of Protestants. The judgment ends in a brief time.

I have gone to Purgatory many times in the company of Saints. The places of expiation are not all in the same state, but in several different ones, and one must go from one to another. On the way, we left behind seas, mountains of ice, snow, clouds. Many times it seems to me that I must descend and go around the world. The Saints approach me easily. They have a pedestal like a luminous cloud that moves with them. These pedestals are of different colors, according to the types of consolation that the Saints procured with their works while they lived.

I must always travel sad paths, but I accept this work in expiation of the sins of the holy souls and I pray for them. Here I recall the sufferings of the Saints and I offer these, together with those of Jesus, for the holy souls.

The states where souls dwell vary greatly according to the state of each. It is possible to compare them to places, which I would call kitchen gardens because, kept in them are certain graces and effects, just as fruits are kept in kitchen gardens. So are the different states in which souls find themselves similar to gardens or mansions, worlds of different types of punishments, miseries, lacks, privations, needs and anguishes.

On arriving at these places I see rays of light that fall on some points or at dusk around the horizon. These are the best. In none of them is a blue sky seen, as everywhere it is more or less disturbed and darkened. In many states souls are very close together, and this causes them much anguish. Some are darker and deeper, other clearer and more elevated.

The spaces where souls are shut in, separated from one another, are also of different forms. Those souls that were united on earth, remain united only if they need to be purified in the same degree. In certain states the light is dyed with the color of a turbid or red fire. The great joy and consolation cannot be expressed of the souls that remain when others are rescued.

I saw that the souls of kings and lords, who during their mortal life tormented others, now served humbly as servants. I saw Protestants in Purgatory who had lived piously in their ignorance. They were abandoned because they lack prayers.

I saw souls that, when others were freed, went up from their lower grade to a higher one. Others I saw that went errantly from one state to another, and could enjoy mutual communication and consolation. A signal grace is to be able to appear to ask for suffrages. I saw places where souls are purified that had been proclaimed Saints, but who on leaving the world had not perfected their holiness.'

Anne Catherine says: 'if one of these could return to the earth, even if for a quarter of an hour, it would cancel many years of punishment in Purgatory.'

Indeed God has given us all the necessary tools required to save our souls from greater suffering. A quarter of an hour in the confessional, with a true repentant heart can save us many years of torment.

THE VIRGIN MARY HELPS
THE SOULS IN PURGATORY

1. Mary helps her servants in Purgatory, says Saint Alphonsus Mary Liguori, Doctor of the Church, in his Treatise on the Most Holy Virgin Mary: *The Glories of Mary.*

'Too happy are the servants of this most kind Mother, since not only in this world they are aided by her, but also in Purgatory they are assisted and consoled by her protection. For succor being there more needed, because they are in torment and cannot help themselves, so much more does this Mother of Mercy strive to help them. Saint Bernadine of Sienna says, that in the prison of souls who are spouses of Jesus Christ, Mary has a certain dominion and plenitude of power to relieve them, as well as to deliver them from their pains.

And, in the first place, in regard to relieving them, the same Saint, applying the words of Ecclesiasticus: I have walked in the waves of the sea: *"In fluctibus maris ambulavi,"* (*Sirach* 24:8), adds, visiting and relieving the necessities and sufferings of my servants, who are my children. He also says that the pains of Purgatory are called waves, because they are transitory, unlike the pains of Hell, which never end. And they are called waves of the sea, because they are very bitter pains. The servants of Mary, tormented by those pains, are often visited and succored by her. See, then, how important it is, – says Novarino, – to be a servant of this good Lady; for she never forgets those who are suffering in flames. And, although Mary succors all the souls in Purgatory, she always obtains more indulgences and alleviations for those who have been especially devoted to her.

The Virgin Mary revealed the following to Saint Bridget:

"I am the Mother of all the souls in Purgatory; and all the sufferings which they merit for the sins committed in life are every hour, while they remain there, alleviated in some measure by my prayers." And this kind Mother sometimes condescends even to enter into that holy prison, to visit and console these, her afflicted children. I have penetrated into the bottom of the deep: '*Profundum abyssi penetravi*' (*Sirach*24:5*).

Applying these words, Saint Bonaventure adds: "I have penetrated the depth of this abyss, that is, of Purgatory, to relieve by my presence those holy souls". "O, how kind and beneficent is the holy Virgin to those who are suffering in Purgatory! – says Saint Vincent Ferrer; through her they receive continual consolation and refreshment."

And what other consolation have they in their sufferings than Mary, and the help of this Mother of Mercy? Saint Bridget one day heard Jesus saying to his Mother: "Thou art my Mother, thou art the Mother of Mercy, thou art the consoler of those who are in Purgatory." And the blessed Virgin herself said to Saint Bridget, that as a poor sick person, suffering and deserted on his bed, feels himself refreshed by some word of consolation, so those souls feel themselves consoled in hearing only her name. The name alone of Mary, a name of hope and salvation, which these beloved children often invoke in that prison, is for them a great comfort. But, then, says Novarino, the loving Mother, on hearing herself invoked by them, adds her prayers to God, by which these souls receive comfort, and find their burning pains cooled as if by dew from Heaven.'

2. Mary Frees Her Servants

But not only does Mary console and succor her servants in Purgatory; she also releases them from their prison, and delivers them by her intercession. From the day of her glorious Assumption, in which that prison is said to have been emptied, as Gerson writes; and Novarino confirms this by saying, that many weighty authors tell that Mary, when about to ascend to Paradise, asked this favor of her Son, that she might take with her all the souls that were then in Purgatory. From that time, says Gerson, the blessed Virgin has possessed the privilege of freeing her servants from those pains. And this also is positively asserted by Saint Bernardine, who says that the blessed Virgin has the power of delivering souls from Purgatory by her prayers and the application of her merits, especially if they have been devoted to her. Novarino reaffirms this, believing that by the merits of Mary, not only are the torments of souls are assuaged, but also abridged. The time of their purgation is shortened by her intercession: and for this it is enough that she presents herself to pray for them.

Saint Peter Damian relates that a certain lady, named Marozia, after death, appeared to her godmother, and told her that on the day of the Assumption of Mary she had been released by her from Purgatory, with a multitude of souls exceeding in number the whole population of Rome. Saint Denis the Carthusian relates that on the festivals of the birth and resurrection of Jesus Christ, Mary descends into Purgatory, accompanied by troops of Angels, and releases many souls from their torments. And Novarino believes that the same thing happens on every solemn festival of the Holy Virgin.

3. Mary Shortens the Time of Purification and Even Cancels It for Her Servants

'Everyone has heard of the promise made by Mary to Pope John XXII, to whom she appeared and ordered him to make known to all those who should wear the sacred scapular of Carmel, that on the Saturday after their death they should be released from Purgatory. And this was proclaimed by the same Pontiff, as Father Cresset relates, in a Bull which he published. It was also confirmed by Alexander V, Clement VII, Pius V, Gregory XII and Paul V, who in a Bull of 1612 said: "That Christians may piously believe that the blessed Virgin will aid by her continual intercession, by her merits and special protection, after death, and principally on Saturday, which is a day consecrated by the Church to the blessed Virgin, the souls of the members of the confraternity of holy Mary of Mount Carmel. Those who have departed this life in the state of grace, worn the scapular, observing chastity according to their state in life, recited the office of the Virgin, and if they had not been able to recite it, shall have observed the fasts of the Church." And in the Solemn Office of the feast of Holy Mary of Mount Carmel, we read that it is piously believed, that the Holy Virgin, with a Mother's love consoles the members of the confraternity of Mount Carmel in Purgatory, and by her intercession conducts them to their heavenly country.

And, why should we not also hope for the same graces and favors, if we are devoted to this good Mother? And if with more special love we serve her, why cannot we hope to obtain the grace of going immediately after death to Paradise, without entering into Purgatory? We read that the holy Virgin said to the blessed Godfrey, through Brother Abondo: "Go and tell brother Godfrey to advance in virtue, for thus he will be a child of my Son, and mine also; and when his soul quits the body, I will not permit it to go to Purgatory, but I will take it and present it to my Son."

And if we would assist the holy souls in Purgatory, let us endeavor to remember them in all our prayers to the blessed Virgin, applying to them especially the holy Rosary, which procures for them great relief.'

4. Apparition of Our Lady at Knock, Ireland

Knock is a small Irish village in County Mayo, with the splendor and greenery of the typical Irish landscape. Knock is surrounded by a heavenly environment, of pure, cold air. It is the place where the Queen of Heaven chose to appear to the grief-stricken people of Ireland. The Mother of God showed, in the most simple, humble, sensitive and radiant way, her profound love for the human race, especially for the deceased faithful.

In 1879, a time when Ireland was going through great social, political and economic difficulties, the 'Great Famine' horrified and devastated the country. The anguished and dejected inhabitants were in despair and did not know what to do and so Reverend Father Cavanagh, the parish priest of Knock, a man of great faith and prayer, decided to celebrate a hundred Masses in honor of the faithful departed, requesting their intercession.

The holy souls did not take long to answer. On the day the priest celebrated the last Mass, something unexpected happened which would change the history of Knock forever. Knock would no longer be the small, unassuming village lost amid the Irish fields, instead it would become one of the most frequented Marian Shrines in the world.

On August 21, at the end of the Eucharistic celebration and in the presence of fifteen faithful, which included men, women and children; Our Lady, Saint Joseph, the Lamb and Saint John the Evangelist appeared, enveloped in radiant light, on the south side of the church.

This silent apparition was of great significance, because there was no visionary given a specific message. But fifteen humble and illiterate eye-witnesses, immediately and without rationalising the event, grasped the message that the Virgin Mary was bringing to the world.

The apparition demonstrates the immense love that the Virgin Mary has for her children in Purgatory.

In His mysterious designs, God invites us urgently to lift our minds and hearts to Him. It is through prayer that we finally encounter His mystery full of wisdom and thus we are truly illumined in the image of Jesus and Mary.

The Eucharist purifies our souls while we go through life; it is a source of grace for our souls and for those that are in Purgatory.

His Holiness, Saint John Paul II, visited this shrine on September 30, 1979, commemorating the centenary of the apparition. Mother Teresa of Calcutta went there also, in 1993.

SAINT MICHAEL THE ARCHANGEL: GUARDIAN OF PURGATORY

Michael: Who is like unto God?

This was the Great Archangel's cry in the battle against Lucifer and the rebellious angels, who were cast into the bottom of the abyss for all eternity. Since then, Michael has been called captain of the heavenly militia.

Saint Michael appears in Sacred Scripture as the guardian, consoler and protector of the people of Israel in times of conflict and affliction. He prepared the return of the Israelites from their captivity in Persia; he led the victory of the courageous Maccabees and rescued Moses' body from the devil's envy.

Since the coming of Christ, the Church has venerated Saint Michael as her special patron and protector.

In Catholic tradition, Saint Michael has four duties

To continue the battle against Satan and the fallen angels.

To rescue the souls of the faithful from the power of Satan, especially at the hour of death.

To protect the People of God: the Jews of the Old Covenant and the Christians of the New Covenant.

To take the souls of the dead and present them to the Lord in their particular judgment and at the end of time in the Last Judgment.

Because of this, Christian iconography depicts him as a soldier, a warrior dressed in armor with a sharp sword, triumphant over a serpent.

The most effective way to glorify Saint Michael in Heaven and on earth, is to recommend devotion to the souls in Purgatory, and to make known the great office he exercises for the suffering souls. God put him in charge of leading the souls that merit Heaven, but are still in the debt of God's justice, to the place of expiation. Where he will introduce them, after their purification, into their eternal dwelling. Every time a soul increases the number of the elect, the good God is glorified by it.

Glory falls on the glorious Prince of Heaven and the glory that the Archangel receives is higher than that of other Saints, because it is proportionate to the greatness of the merits of the one who receives it, as well as the value of the act that has merited such recompense. Jesus said: 'to him who has, more shall be given!'

It is a great honor for Saint Michael to present souls to the Lord that sing His mercies, and to unite their gratitude to that of the elect for all eternity. When the good God allows it, we can communicate directly with the Archangel, in the same way the spirits and souls of the blessed communicate among themselves.

They are unable to make us understand all the love that the heavenly Archangel has for us. He gives us encouragement in our suffering **(it is a soul in Purgatory speaking),** speaking to us from Heaven. We see Saint Michael as the Angels are seen in their angelic nature. He does not have a body. He comes to Purgatory to relieve all the most purified souls. He is the first among the first princes in incomparable greatness and glory.

Our Guardian Angels also comes to visit us in this place of punishment, but Saint Michael exceeds all of them in beauty and majesty. The Virgin Most Holy descends into Purgatory on her feast days and she returns to Heaven with many souls. While she is with us, no one suffers: Saint Michael accompanies his Queen faithfully, but when he comes alone or accompanied by an Angel, we all suffer as usual.

Tell confessors that if they wish to do something pleasing for Saint Michael, that should they recommend incessant devotion to the souls in Purgatory. You must say that, the Purgatory of consecrated persons or those who have received more graces, is longer and much more painful than that of ordinary souls.

The most effective means of relieving souls is to order a Holy Mass to be celebrated or heard devoutly, the *Via Crucis* and the Holy Rosary, which includes the life and death of Jesus and Mary (1).

Appearing to one of his favorite devotees – the Servant of God Antonia de Astona, of Portugal – Saint Michael said to her that he wanted to be honored with an angelic chaplet having nine salutations to each one of the angelic choirs (See chapter *Prayers and Suffrages*).

Saint Michael promised that whoever prays this chaplet every day, will enjoy in life his special protection and after death will be released from Purgatory. He added also that during Holy Communion an angel will be assigned to him from each choir, to accompany him at the Sacred Table (2).

PERSONAL REVELATION: MYSTICAL EXPERIENCE OF PURGATORY

MARINO RESTREPO

It would be impossible for me to describe my experience of Purgatory exactly as it happened, or explain to you, the mystery of all that occurred. But the Holy Spirit who is the one, who makes it possible for a supernatural event to be presented in natural language, will be in charge of expressing, in the depth of the hearts of those who read these lines, all that I cannot do humanly.

During Christmas in 1997, I was visiting my native country, Colombia. At midnight on the 25th of December, on entering the property of an uncle of mine in Anserma, Caldas, the coffee region where I was born, I was intercepted and kidnapped by a group of FARC guerrillas. They bound me, covered my head and took me deep into the Forest of the Pacific. I was in captivity for a total of six months. For the first fifteen days I was kept in a cave, deep in the forest, until a second group of guerrillas arrived to take me further into the jungle, to ensure my concealment while they decided on a ransom. The cave was unbearably humid and full of bats and all sorts of bugs and insects; I was fed only once a day with roots, and forest fruits since it was the only food available from the surrounding terrain.

I was born in the heart of a Catholic family and was educated in all the values, Doctrine and Tradition of the Church. At 14 I began to distance myself from the Catholic faith, influenced by the 60s culture, I left the faith. In that cave

I did not have the smallest understanding of my spiritual unction. I had been away from God for 33 years. I did not know how to pray and I had no sense of spiritual reflection which would lead me to repent.

On the fifteenth day I was sentenced to death. My captors asked me for a very large sum of money and threatened to kill my family if I was unable to pay. They refused to spare my life and the following night they tied me up again, covered my head, and shoved me into the cave. It is difficult to describe what I went through that night; I felt anguish, despair and an intense agony that welled up from the depth of my being. I could not cry or shout, despite how much I wished to do so, all my strength had been drained from me. I felt a deep sense of futility and emptiness inside; it was as if I ceased to exist.

At that moment, something extraordinarily mysterious happened. Being both completely awake and conscious, I began to recall my life in detail from the age of three. I was experiencing two realities simultaneously: at 47 in that cave, and reliving my childhood. My first instinct was to run outside, but I knew that the guerrillas would kill me, thinking that I was trying to escape. I had no choice but to stay in the cave and live out that unfathomable mystery. Throughout the night, for some eight or nine hours, I had a mystical experience that transformed my life for good. Since then, I have never been the same.

The Lord Jesus revealed to me the mysteries I had inherited from the Catholic Church through my parents faith, which I had abandoned, rejected or ignored for so many years. It would take me years to recount all that I lived through that night mystically, but in a brief presentation of this experience, I will concentrate only on what concerns Purgatory. Although I also experienced Hell that night and the reality of earthly life seen from the Spirit of God, in the person of Jesus Christ, His Son.

After reliving my life since infancy, an *illumination of my conscience* given that I experienced it while was awake in the cave and going through terrible pains, which were not physical, but profoundly and mysteriously spiritual. I am certain they were the pains of my sins. I was taken to what appeared to be a plain of the spirit, a state of existence that God alone has complete knowledge of, it cannot be explained. I was on a very high mountain with my face on the ground, amid perfect silence. As I looked up, in the distance, I could see another mountain of even greater magnitude; it was as if new dimensions were being unfolded before me. On the great mountain ahead of me I became aware of the most beautiful city, enveloped extraordinarily in light. Despite the distance between the two mountains, I could see the city perfectly and my soul knew that I should have arrived there, but was unable to do so. Throughout this experience I was in a perfect state of consciousness; I understood everything very clearly without needing anyone to explain it to me. It was only some time after this event, that I was able to deduce that it has been the work of the Holy Spirit.

On the mountain I heard a voice speaking to me; it was so immense: it came from the innermost depths of the universe, and from deep within my very being. It was a voice full of love, of compassion; I desperately wanted to melt into its great mercy, but my soul could not bear it. It was thoroughly darkened by sin and it could not endure that very pure, perfect love. I rejected that love; it was the Lord's voice I was hearing. Suddenly, He fell silent, He no longer spoke to me and I was immersed in indescribable darkness.

Everything vanished: the mountains, the city of light, the Lord's voice. By rejecting that love which will not impose itself, I remained separated from His grace. The pain caused by the absence of His love was so great that my soul remained floating over an abyss of darkness, in which I was sure it would disintegrate. It was a bottomless abyss. I knew where I was but I did not want to face it. I had lived for 33 years in mortal sin, far from God, separated from His Church. I had denied the existence of Hell and I knew at that moment that I was floating over it.

Today I can attest with my life that Hell exists. This belief does not stem from something I read in a book, or believed from the teachings of the Catechism of the Catholic Church, but because I have lived it. Indeed as a child, I ridiculed the very idea of Hell and denied its existence. Yet in God's infinite Mercy he revealed to me the darkness of Hell, and so only God can comprehend how it was possible for me to experience it.

I felt as if the experience of Hell lasted for an eternity; later on the Lord spoke to me again and I returned to the same mountain, face down in the grass, where I had rejected the Lord's voice. After speaking to me for a long time about humanity, future and past events, and giving me an immensely beautiful presentation of the Catholic Church, as the continuation of Judaism and the only Church of God. He revealed to me the reason why he created me a Catholic. He explained that to be a Catholic, is to be a Eucharistic instrument of reparation. I could never articulate the pain I felt when He revealed to me the number of souls that could have been saved during 33 years of my life, had I been faithful to Him.

He revealed to me the mystical depth of the Sacraments, the Sacred Traditions of the Church, and the saving Doctrine. He showed me so much about the Church that I was absolutely enriched and enraptured by the wonders we have inherited.

I then appeared in a lake with the water up to my waist. In front of the lake I could see a beautiful rock which, despite the distance (which in earthy measures could be the distance between the earth and the sun) I saw perfectly, and I knew instantly that Jesus would appear to me in that rock. I was also acutely aware that I would not be able to look at Him because of my sinful state. At that moment, I tried to sink into the lake to flee from His presence, but I discovered that I was standing in the midst of all my sins. 33 years of sin surrounded me, and each sin was directly linked with an evil spirit that was still very active in my life. My soul was in a state of Purgatory. All those years of sin were marked clearly by the presence of all the evil spirits I had associated with. I can only tell you that my purgatorial state had to be a state very close to the mouth of Hell. Only God's Mercy prevented me from being consumed forever in eternal fire.

When I looked at one of the spirits, I relived that sin perfectly as if it were the first time I had committed it. I lived the entire sequence again as if I were alive. First the temptation, followed swiftly by the moment of consent, and finally the consequence of that sin. I saw how that sin affected my whole family, generations to come, the souls in Purgatory and the entire Church. The inextricable bonds formed between sin, soul and spirit were revealed. This caused me immense pain and the further I penetrated into the dimension of the spirits, the more complex, sophisticated and intense this intrinsic relationship became. I could feel within my whole being the very grave wound that each sin had inflicted on me and what in Hell, was a permanent deformation of the soul, converted into a demonised being – a monster. In Purgatory, those consequences of sin appear as grave wounds which are going through a painful healing, a purification, a purgation, if it can be explained thus. And all this for long periods in where the soul may dwell in various dimensions of suffering, depending on the rigor and the time given to each sin. Something like, when a person is wounded after a serious car accident, one knows, that despite their 'monstrous' appearance, the gashes and swelling will disappear and they will return to normal once they have completely healed.

The healing is not only the pain of having offended God with the evil committed, and knowing the dimensional consequence of each sin, but also the interminable series of states that must be endured. Extreme cold, heat, desert; alternating locations, between what seem to be caverns, tunnels and abysses; rough terrains full of thorns and depressing landscapes of grey and discolored yellow. These are states where one feels that the soul enters an abysmal solitude, an intense desire to advance towards the light.

I could see souls that seemed to be enveloped in gauze and one could see only small areas of their physiognomy. Their appearance varied between something such as wood, very cold metal or fire that seemed to emerge from within. I could see clearly the ascent of these states towards the fullness of light. It is an immense suffering that also swims in immense hope. Despite so much pain there is a mysterious state of love in the souls, which is so great that it could only be described as the pain of desiring, with all one's being, total perfection and complete holiness, which is still in the distance, but already an attainable reality. It is not easy to explain how it is possible, in the midst of such great sufferings, for a soul to live with so much hope and with a desire to attain the fullness of eternal joy and the infinite peace of God, without despair and without any sign of rebellion or rejection against the suffering. Despite having all the characteristics I describe, I cannot say that it is the same physical state that I know of the material world. Everything looks like it, but it is not the same. It is light years ahead of our understanding. All the landscapes and different areas through which the suffering soul is purified, which I have described briefly, exist as if they were the pedagogic scenery of God' Love which continues molding souls towards perfection. Although for the soul, it is far from being simple scenery, indeed it is a reality that molds and corrects, that makes one aware and deepens each act of enmity, converting it into light.

As the soul advances in these states toward the light, it is increasingly embellished and the immense joy it begins to radiate, is converted into a light, that is more brilliant than that of the stars of the heavenly firmament. The light of souls, which enter into the plenitude of the glory of God, cannot be compared with what we know in the material world; the light of the sun is a poor reflection of what the light of eternity is.

My first experience on seeing myself in this state of Purgatory was, perhaps, that of the lowest level, because I could feel the anguish of being in such darkness and in the presence of so many evil spirits. Their presence forced me to experience areas that I had already lived in Hell. I knew, however, that it was not Hell, but the pain I felt was similar in intensity. The presence of evil was very different in Purgatory, because one no longer felt enslaved to the forces of darkness, or to the infernal strength of a fire that sprang from the lowest part of the abyss and pierced all souls. However, simply being in the midst of those evil presences was sufficient for the soul to be tormented on discovering, and feeling the profundity of every act of disobedience to God and of every act of enmity.

The degrees of a soul's darkness, which is sin caused by the absence of God's love, vary in dimensions of consequence and intensity. These are dimensions in which one lives the purification or purgation. I am sure that the gravest of sins will sink the suffering soul practically to the doors of the abyss, inflicting it with enormous pains and long stays in Purgatory, in very many cases until the end of time. Whilst I am not sure whether sins of impurity are the gravest, or even amongst the gravest of sins committed. I experienced the reality of Purgatory as a soul stained with the sins of impurity

I am convinced that each soul is unique, and the personal judgment of each at the moment of death, is also unique. However all sins that violate God's Law documented in the Ten Commandments and which, are considered to be mortal sins by the Church, would appear to be treated to the same severity and intensity of purification.

Both the term, and consequence of 'mortal sin' is dangerously unobserved, indeed there is a severe lack of sufficiently profound, direct and effective catechesis for souls regarding this reality. There is not enough reflection on it to pierce the hardness of sin and reach the depth of the conscience. Yet ignorance of mortal sin is the key to long periods of suffering and purgation before you will be able to face the divinity of Christ.

I was able to relive before the Lord Jesus a sin of adultery, that was justified by the dramatisation of a theatrical piece. This happened in Hamburg, Germany, at the beginning of the 70s. I appeared in the cafeteria of the University of Hamburg where I was studying Fine Arts; I was in a conversation with an actress with whom I was to work and perform alongside in scenes of a sexual nature. It was a classic German piece of Eighteenth Century theatre. The two of us had complete control over the levels of intimacy presented on stage. However, during our discussions about the performance, I saw how easily we were tempted to engage in a sinful act. In a matter of minutes a very evil and impure environment had been created between us and though it was completely unnecessary, we agreed to consummate the sexual act on stage before a public audience.

The Lord showed me the reality of the spirit when man unites himself in marriage to his wife and becomes one flesh, united with God so that, open to life, they can be instruments of procreation for the economy of salvation. The impure act I participated in was an unholy union, antithetical to that of marriage and spiritual unification with God. My sin of impurity, an act of adultery since I was a married man, was an offence to God and a mortal sin. I was shown that flesh which unites itself in a sin of impurity is united, not in blessing, but in damnation. The Lord revealed to me the reality of this damnation; I saw myself appear, united to that woman in one flesh, as a monster, with four arms, four legs, and two heads; I looked like a Hindu deity. It was a horror to see myself so and to feel the pain of being unable to separate my soul from the deformed being; this was a state in which the soul would have to suffer for a long time, whilst detaching itself from the other.

The mystery of this manifestation lies in the different states of the two souls that sinned together: one of the two being still in the flesh and the other already in the presence and judgment of God. Both souls are united in their sin and so if the second soul, on dying, was also in a state of mortal sin, having made no confession or reparation for the act, they would partake in a similar suffering.

In addition to the sin we both bore for the performance on stage, we also bore the sins of the entire audience at each showings, of which there were nine. I was able to see, through the infusion of the Holy Spirit, the way each individual in the audience was affected by the impurity of the sin and the effect of the evil spirits at work. I observed how those spirits moved among the audience, fueled by scenes on stage, gaining strength among the audience, and increasing in passion like a tempest.

The vision of this sin was so immense, that I could see how the corporal language of the audience became more intense, and transformed as the work progressed. Those women, who were already attacked by the spirits of impurity, and dressed seductively, became the center of everyone's attention. I saw it was a calculated strategy of evil intended to exacerbate sinful urges and build a momentum of desire. The atmosphere was that of an explicit concert of what could be viewed as a massive sexual act between the actors and the public. The eyes of all the people were like red torches that changed in intensity and moved between the actors and the sexual scene, trying to locate themselves in a person or persons of the public. Indeed the spirits awakened a thirst that needed to be satiated in everyone. I cannot even imagine what an hour pornographic film could generate. It is very possible that it would lead a soul to the very door of Hell if it did not repent in time.

My sins were alive before the Lord because I lived for 33 years without the sacrament of Confession. If I had died the night I had the mystical experience with God, it would only be His Mercy that saved me and sent me to Purgatory, with the knowledge that I would need to spend a long period of time there to be healed and make reparation.

Purgatory is a state of God's Mercy, an antechamber to his Glory. Throughout the Gospel, Jesus insists on inviting us to transcend from this life, to the eternal, directly to Heaven, and he has given us all the weapons and tools we need to do it.

Purgatory is an experience unique to each soul, not all souls purged of a certain sin are in the same desert of cold, heat or any other state determined by that particular sin. I discovered the innumerable purgatorial levels and I saw thousands, upon thousands of souls dwelling on the same level, yet I was able to see that each soul lives its own Purgatory. The best comparison I can make with what I wish to express as the 'state of soul,' would be to ask a person what he thinks or feels about the city where he lives. In other words:

his experience of that city. We can be sure that if we interviewed a hundred people in the same city, even members of the same family or household, each one would have a unique experience of life in that city. So much so, that they could be describing completely different cities. These are interior states, very intimate to the being, which are created or penetrated through experiences.

If we relate this analogy to sin, then we can appreciate that depending on an individual's experience of sin, the soul on dying, will gradually display the many dimensions of disorder, uniquely created by their sins (sin being a state of disorder in relation to God's Law, which is unique to each soul). Therefore such an experience of Purgatory is unique, and so we can conceive the mystery of the various dimensions a soul will live in Purgatory.

On leaving the body the soul is fixed in the same state it was at the moment it left. The state of the soul at that point is determined by a life's formation, in which the events experienced and choices made have molded and deformed the soul. There is no way of changing anything once the soul leaves the material body. That is why the Church teaches us that during the time in the flesh, we are in the Mercy of God. Once we leave the flesh, we are in His Justice.

A soul that has been saved and is in Purgatory, will go deeper into a purification as it resolves each event lived, that occurred without love and without reparation. True reparation is made through the Sacrament of Reconciliation, where sins are forgiven and absolved, and by good works and a sincere change of heart.

The Christianity of Protestantism and all sects, particularly those founded in the United Kingdom is removed from the roots of sacred traditions, and it consequently is divorced from which are directed by Scottish Freemasonry and York rites; such as the Evangelicals, the Pentecostals, the Baptists, the Adventists, the Presbyterians and the Anglicans, as well as the hundreds upon hundreds of Christian sects derived from them, created generally in North America.

Sects and Christian denominations, which are focused on prosperity, physical healing and spiritual deliverance, are a blend of various religious beliefs and practices. They have no root in sacred tradition and unlike Catholicism, they are no longer a Judeo- Christian faith since they have sprung from the spiritual heritage of Judaism.

This kind of Christianity, which we could call the most astute propagation of New Age, cannot conceive the existence of Purgatory. Because of spiritual arrogance and pride, these denominations lost the humility necessary for reconciliation.

They rejected and ignored the Eucharistic Jesus, the Bread of Eternal Life and Body and Blood of the Lord. By doing they have separated themselves from a sanctifying grace which purifies the soul.

In my experience of Purgatory, I was able to see the thousands upon thousands of Christian souls from these sects who, because they lived a considerably good life, attained the mercy of purification, and were in Purgatory. The only prayers raised to Heaven for their souls are those of the Catholic Church; in the daily Masses for the souls in Purgatory, especially those in greatest need of God's Mercy. Otherwise, no one would pray for them. Souls that are saved but which suffer more intense purification, are those of Catholics who converted to Protestantism.

Others are the souls of Catholics who are seduced by human science and intellectual properties neglecting the graces of Baptism and their Christian mission. Those that are saved go through very difficult states of recognition of these ignored truths and squandered works of love. Worship of the intellect, of intelligence, of culture; fascination with human talents have severe consequences for the soul, because they plunge it into a false spiritual sphere. The essence of God's true love is diluted in an ocean of superfluous fantasies. When the soul leaves the body and is detached from the material world, it enters the fullness of the spiritual world and regrets not having spent its earthly time nourishing itself spiritually and failing to grow in God.

Every act of unconditional love for one's neighbor is an immortal act; it is the true health of the soul; it exists only on the love of God. At the end of this life, such a soul will have as much spiritual health as it loved with the love of God, a selfless love that gives all, expecting nothing in return. Many souls are in Purgatory enduring painful punishments for failing to do reparation for inimical acts, acts which they were unaware of in life. There are many areas of our conduct that have been lived without love. Our humanity becomes insensitive to the love of God, separating the soul from its eternal salvation. It costs much to rescue it in Purgatory.

Vital is the time that God gives us to provide our soul with spiritual food, so that it will be prepared, forged in Eternal Love and ascend from the darkness of the earthly exile to the heights of light. Each instant counts. Just as a pregnant woman takes care of the development of her baby and hopes that the baby is not born prematurely or malnourished, so should we look after the health of our soul. We bear our soul in the flesh, which is mortal. At the moment of death, when our soul leaves our body, our spiritual destiny is defined eternally

If a person is not conscious of this spiritual reality; if there is no coherence between the material and the spiritual, but attains eternal salvation by Divine Mercy, he will have to undergo purgation and acquire the love that he lacked. Only then will he be able to enter the Divine Shrine of eternal glory. The more we are immersed in today's materialism, the more souls will necessarily have to pass through Purgatory and, inevitably, many will be condemned, more than at other times.

It is frequently argued that we live Hell, Purgatory or Heaven here on earth. If we raise this argument to the spirit, we could say that during our earthly life we build and form the eternal state of our soul. Therefore, if we live in obedience to God, acting in love, goodness and humility, we will grow in sanctifying grace. Without such grace we will not enter our heavenly dwelling.

If we choose to live in an unstable relationship with God and refuse to take responsibility for our sinfulness, we are building ourselves a sure path to Purgatory. We must rise up from mediocrity and lukewarm faith. We must act only with the Love of God towards our neighbor and work tirelessly to secure the salvation of souls. After our death our soul will have to expiate the imperfection of its acts, not having sufficient light to rise to the heights of the Divine Shrine and the House of the Heavenly Father immediately after we die.

To rise in the light, is to challenge our weaknesses daily and to focus our whole life, 24 hours a day, on struggling to attain holiness. We must seek perfection in every act; in every intention of our heart, in every emotion, sentiment, passion, thought or plan. A life lived like this, with perseverance, patience and humbleness, where we acknowledge our limitations and sinfulness, will lead us to great heights at the end of our earthly life.

If we were to live a life separated from the love of God, we would easily fall prey to the darkness of sin. We would be demonised in life; our soul would be darkened and our heart would be hardened (Saint Augustine, Sermon 169, 11, 13) sinking forever into the abyss of darkness, condemned to Hell, unable to endure the light and love of God for having preferred the darkness of sin.

The Catechism says this about the existence of Hell:

1034. 'Jesus often speaks of "Gehenna," of "the unquenchable fire" reserved for those who to the end of their lives refuse to believe and be converted, where both soul and body can be lost. Jesus solemnly proclaims that he "will send his angels, and they will gather [...] all evil doers, and throw them into the furnace of fire" (*Matthew* 13:41-42) and that he will pronounce the condemnation: "Depart from me, you cursed, into the eternal fire!" '(*Matthew* 25:41).

This is what Article 8 of the Catechism of the Catholic Church says about sin:

Mercy and Sin

1846. ' The Gospel is the revelation in Jesus Christ of God's Mercy to sinners (cf. *Luke* 15). The angel announced to Joseph: "You shall call his name Jesus, for he will save his people from their sins' (*Matthew* 1:21). And in the institution of the Eucharist, Sacrament of Redemption, Jesus says: "This is my blood of the covenant, which is poured out for many for the forgiveness of sins" ' (*Matthew* 26:28).

1847. " God created us without us: but he did not will to save us without us" (Saint Augustine, Sermon 169, 11, 13). The reception of his Mercy calls for the confession of our faults. "If we say we have no sin, we deceive ourselves, and the truth is not in us. If we confess our sins, he is faithful and just, and will forgive our sins and cleanse us from all unrighteousness" (1 *John* 1:8-9).

Definition of Sin

1849. ' Sin is an offense against reason, truth and right conscience; it is failure in genuine love of God and neighbor caused by a perverse attachment to certain goods. It wounds the nature of man and injures human solidarity. It has been defined as "an utterance, a deed or a desirer contrary to the eternal law" '(Saint Augustine, Faust. 22, 27; Saint Thomas Aquinas, S. Th., 1-2, 71, 6).

1857. ' For a *sin to be mortal*, three conditions must together be met: "Mortal sin is sin whose object of grave matter and which is also committed with full knowledge and deliberate consent" ' (RP 17).

1858. '*Grave matter* is specified by the Ten Commandments, corresponding to the answer of Jesus to the rich young man: "Do not kill, Do not commit adultery, Do not steal, Do not bear false witness, Do not defraud, Honor your father and your mother" (*Mark* 10:19). The gravity of sins is more or less great: murder is graver than theft. One must also take into account who is wronged: violence against parents is in itself graver than violence against a stranger.'

1859. 'Mortal sin requires *full knowledge* and *complete consent*. It presupposes knowledge of the sinful character of the act, of its opposition to God's law. It also implies a consent sufficiently deliberate to be a personal choice. Feigned ignorance and hardness of heart do not diminish, but rather increase, the voluntary character of sin.'

The Church teaches us that the soul can separate itself radically from God by its own will and condemn itself. It is a reality that is conveniently ignored in today's world, instead the world has become open to libertinage.

It is very common today, even in some Catholic pastorals, to evade the catechesis on the states of Heaven, Purgatory and Hell. I have had the sad opportunity of hearing homilies where the existence of Hell, as well as of Purgatory, has been denied.

Why are there more souls going to Hell and Purgatory today? Why have these modern theologies dedicated themselves to preaching only the 'Mercy' of God and that all of us, without exception, will go to Heaven at the end of this life? Because materialism and relativism have won us over, and we have combined today's currents in such a way, that it seems as if the globalisation of our world has also globalised our religion. It seems to have transformed into a Buddhist and Hindu image; into a New Age mixture, in which we find some Catholic Orders practicing all sorts of Eastern pagan customs. Combining New Age philosophies with the Doctrine of our faith.

Liberation Theology, modern psychologies, techniques to overcome self, Orientalism, superstition and a huge area of alternative medicines, are a sure ticket to Purgatory for Catholics involved in such things: all this being a consequence of *"syncretism"*.

We, as Catholics, have a huge responsibility to live our faith exactly as it has been revealed to us by our Lord Jesus Christ. Our Catholic Church is the Church of the Lord Jesus, and in his doctrine, he reveals to us all the mysteries that will provide us with the sanctifying grace of eternal salvation in Jesus Christ. Everything has already been given to us. We have no excuse if we fail in our own salvation and the salvation of the souls that God puts on our path.

Purgatory really exists. How great it would be if all Catholics believed in this reality, because many would avoid the painful purification of Purgatory and work more arduously for purification in this life. May the Father of our Lord Jesus Christ have mercy on all of us and grant us eternal salvation.

'The Soul Enamored with the Child Jesus' : Blessed Lawrence Mary of Saint Francis of Saverio.

November 2

The Child Jesus speaks: *Son, may the sacred sound of the bells revive in you the desire to pray for your brothers who are in Purgatory. For these prayers, you will obtain my kingdom, as there are many souls who are in need of your help.*

The special Virtue to practice on this day will be: to pray for the souls in Purgatory. Amen.

Prayer: My Child Jesus, I am willing to pray for all the needy souls in Purgatory. Amen.

On doing the dishes, the Venerable Francis of the Child Jesus, a Carmelite, certain that she would be heard, prayed to the Child Jesus for the release of a soul from Purgatory. On Christmas Eve of 1716, the Venerable M. Serio saw the Child Jesus, who allowed her to hear the clamor of the souls in Purgatory.

Practice: The dead cry out for your help. Offer a Mass for them.

Short Prayer: Divine Child Jesus, You are my treasure.

PRAYERS AND SUFFRAGES

It is a work of mercy to pray and offer sacrifices for the holy souls in Purgatory, especially the sacrifice of the Holy Mass. It is the balm that we, as the Militant Church, can offer for them to attenuate the pain of their punishment, until they attain eternal glory. Each prayer, sacrifice or offering we do for them is of the greatest importance. It is through these acts that we help them to come closer to their definitive encounter with the Highest Good. This is the reason souls are so grateful to us. Our prayer means everything to them, as they can no longer gain merits themselves. It is important to understand that only God knows when a soul has attained the fullness of glory. Therefore, we must not neglect or abandon our prayer for souls. If they have already attained glory, those prayers are received by another soul in need of them. No prayer goes unanswered.

The holy souls benefit greatly, especially from the Holy Sacrifice of the Mass, for which we have many testimonies. We can also see that, after a specific number of Masses have been said for a soul, it completes the expiation of its sins and goes to eternal joy. The Holy Rosary is another way to help souls. By praying it with much attention and devotion, souls receive many graces through the Most Holy Virgin Mary. Devotion to the Divine Mercy is also a great relief for souls in such need. In many of Saint Faustina's experiences, narrated in the pages of her book, she tells us how souls benefit greatly from the recitation of the Divine Mercy chaplet.

In the Divine Mercy novena, the eighth day is dedicated to the souls in Purgatory, full prayer for the eighth below:

1226. Today bring to Me the souls who are in the prison of Purgatory, and immerse them in the abyss of My mercy. Let the torrents of My Blood cool down their scorching flames. All these souls are greatly loved by Me. They are making retribution to My justice. It is in your power to bring them relief. Draw all the indulgences from the treasury of My Church and offer them on their behalf. Oh, if you only knew the torments they suffer, you would continually offer for them the alms of the spirit and pay off their debt to My justice.

1227. Most Merciful Jesus, You Yourself have said that You desire mercy; so I bring into the abode of Your Most Compassionate Heart the souls in Purgatory, souls who are very dear to You, and yet, who must make retribution to Your justice. May the streams of Blood and Water which gushed forth from Your Heart put out the flames of Purgatory, that there, too, the power of Your mercy may be celebrated. From the terrible heat of the fire of Purgatory a lament is raised to Your Mercy. And they receive consolation, relief and refreshment in the torrent of Blood and Water shed.

Eternal Father, turn your merciful gaze upon the souls suffering in Purgatory, who are enfolded in the Most Compassionate Heart of Jesus. I beg you, by the sorrowful Passion of Jesus Your Son, and by all the bitterness with which His most sacred Soul was flooded. Manifest your mercy to the souls who are under Your just scrutiny. Look upon them in no other way but only through the Wounds of Jesus, Your dearly beloved Son; for we firmly believe that there is no limit to Your goodness and compassion.

Offering up sacrifices is a very effective way of helping souls. If we endure a personal hardship, sickness or simply something we do not like, we are dying to ourselves, and the offering of this act is the eternal life of souls. Every time we pray or offer up a sacrifice to assist souls, we aid them in their release from Purgatory and increase the number of souls in Heaven who adore and praise God.

Sacred Catholic Traditions teach us different ways to pray for souls. There are so many ways to do this. Here we mention a few, that teach us how to unite ourselves with the suffering Church.

Saint Gregory the Great, Supreme Pontiff and Doctor of the Church, left a very important legacy regarding souls in Purgatory: the Gregorian Masses and the nine prayers for souls.

The name *Gregorian Masses* is taken from Saint Gregory the Great who was Pope from 590 to 604. He contributed to the spread of the pious practice which celebrated Masses for the release of souls in Purgatory. In his writings, he tells us that he celebrated Masses for 30 days for the eternal repose of the soul of Justus, a monk who died in the monastery of Saint Andrew in Rome. At the end of the last Mass, the deceased appeared to one of his fellow monks telling him that he had been released from the flames of Purgatory.

The Gregorian Masses are a series of Masses that are traditionally offered for 30 consecutive days, as soon as possible after a person's death. These Masses are offered individually for a person's soul.

The important custom of celebrating Gregorian Masses for a soul immediately after a persons death confirms the need for a great deal of intercessory prayer, on death, for recently departed souls to gain passage to Heaven.

Indeed the intercessory power of Christ's sacrifice, present in the Holy Mass, is of the greatest relief to a recently departed and suffering soul. The immense power from the offering of the Mass helps the recently departed soul to continue in its perfection through grace, which will enable it to enter, into union with our God, who is love itself.

The Nine Prayers of Saint Gregory the Great for the Souls in Purgatory

First Prayer
O my Lord, Jesus Christ, who to redeem me were scourged, crowned with thorns and crucified! I adore You and beg You that your cross may defend me from the evil enemy.

Our Father, Hail Mary, Glory be.

Second Prayer
O my Lord, Jesus Christ, who to redeem me went through so many torments and drank gall and vinegar! I adore You and beg You that those torments may be the remedy of my soul

Our Father, Hail Mary, Glory be.

Third Prayer

O my Lord, Jesus Christ, by the bitterness that You suffered for my sins on the cross, mainly in the hour that Your noble soul was separated from your Sacred Body, I beg You to have mercy on my soul when it leaves this world.

Our Father, Hail Mary, Glory be.

Fourth Prayer

O my Lord, Jesus Christ, who to redeem me Your Sacred Body was anointed with myrrh, embalmed and placed in the sepulcher! I adore You and beg You that Your death may be my life.

Our Father, Hail Mary, Glory be.

Fifth Prayer

O my Lord, Jesus Christ, who descended into Purgatory and Limbo, and rescued those who were captive there! I adore You and beg You, do not let my soul be captive in Hell.

Our Father, Hail Mary, Glory be.

Sixth Prayer

O my Lord, Jesus Christ, who with Your power You resurrected and ascended to Heaven, where You are seated at the right hand of the Father! I beg You to have mercy on me!

Our Father, Hail Mary, Glory be.

Seventh Prayer

O my Lord, Jesus Christ, Good Shepherd! Defend the just, give light to sinners, have mercy on the deceased faithful and be gentle with me who is a great sinner.

Our Father, Hail Mary, Glory be.

Eighth Prayer

O my Lord, Jesus Christ, who will come to judge us to take the just to glory, crown them in it and send the wicked away to Hell! I adore You and beg You that Your Passion may free me from all punishment and take me to eternal life.

Our Father, Hail Mary, Glory be.

Ninth Prayer

O Most Beloved Father! I offer You the Innocent Death of your Son and the love of His Divine Heart for the punishments that I, the greatest sinner, deserve for my faults; I offer You, also, his Passion and Divine Love, for all my relatives and friends, enemies and those entrusted to me; have mercy on them.

Our Father, Hail Mary, Glory be.

Offering

I offer these prayers through the merits of the Passion and Death of our Lord Jesus Christ, whom I beg to receive them in atonement for my sins; and I ask our Lord to release from Purgatory, a soul for His great glory and that of the Most Holy Virgin Mary, whom I beg to be my advocate with your Divine Majesty.

The One Hundred *Requiems*

Many graces, it is said, have been obtained through the mediation of the holy souls in Purgatory through this Carmelite devotion of the One Hundred *Requiems*.

This good practice consists of ten Our Fathers and one hundred *requiems*. A five-decade Rosary can be used for this, which is to be said twice, to make up the one hundred. It begins with the sign of the cross, followed by the Act of Contrition. One Our Father and then ten *requiems*, saying ten times:

Eternal rest grant onto them O Lord and let Perpetual Light shine upon them.

At the end of the ten *requiems*, the following invocations are said:

Holy souls, patient souls, captive souls, pray to God for us, as we pray for you so that the Lord will give you his glory. Eternal Father, I offer you the Blood, Passion and Death of Our Lord Jesus Christ, the sorrows of the Most Holy Virgin and those of Saint Joseph, for the remission of our sins, the release of souls from Purgatory and the conversion of sinners.

The ten decades prayed thus, with the invocations at the end of each one of them, complete the one hundred *requiems*. Pope Leo XIII granted each *requiem* fifty days of indulgence.

Saint Gertrude's Prayer

Our Lord told Saint Gertrude that the following prayer would release one thousand souls from Purgatory every time it is said devoutly.

Eternal Father, I offer Thee the Most Precious Blood of Thy Divine Son, Jesus, in union with the masses said throughout the world today, for all the holy souls in purgatory, for sinners everywhere, for sinners in the universal church, those in my own home and within my family. Amen.

Maremagnum

Great sea of indulgences is written with lead writing in the Pontiff's palace.

Every time it is recited innumerable indulgences are gained.

O highest cross! O innocent and precious blood! O great and cruel punishment! O poverty of Christ my Redeemer! O very painful wounds! O pierced heart! O bitter death of God! O great dignity of God worthy of being reverenced! Help me, Lord, to attain eternal life, now and at the hour of my death. Amen.

The Fifteen Prayers revealed by Our Lord to Saint Bridget of Sweden in the Church of Saint Paul in Rome

Published under sanction of the Decree of November 18, 1966; published in the *Apostolicae Sedis* Act, Tome 58, Number 16 of December 29, 1966.

Pope Benedict XV expressed himself as follows on the revelation of Saint Bridget:

'The approbation of such revelations implies nothing more than, after mature examination, it is permissible to publish them for the unit of the faithful. Though they don't merit the same credence as the truths of religion, one can, however, believe them out of human faith, conforming to the rules of prudence by which they are probable, and supported by sufficient motives that one might believe in them piously.'

These prayers and promises were copied from a book printed in Toulouse, France, in 1740. They were published by Father Adrien Parvilliers of the Society of Jesus. Father Adrien was a Jesuit, apostolic missionary in the Holy Land and he obtained the approval and permission to spread these prayers.

Fathers of families, men and women teachers, who teach these prayers to little ones for at least a year, will be rewarded by God. This promise is applied equally to those who facilitate them to others. They are assured the privilege of being spared during life from every serious accident that could cause the loss of one of their five senses.

Pope Pius IX acknowledged the authenticity of these prayers for the good of souls; he signed the approval on May 31, 1862.

To obtain the *Privileges* it is necessary to recite the prayers every day without interruption. However, if for a grave reason a day is missed, the *Privileges* will not be lost. One should begin again reciting the prayers daily for the entire year. Supposing that during the complete year 5480 prayers are recited, everything will remain intact on completing what was missing. One must pray with devotion, concentrating on the words pronounced.

Those who visit Saint Paul's Church in Rome can still contemplate the Miraculous Crucifix placed above the Tabernacle, which is found in the Chapel of the Most Holy Sacrament. This Miraculous Crucifix was sculpted by Pierre Cavallini. It is the same one before which Saint Bridget knelt when she received these 15 Prayers directly from Our Lord. Moreover, in that same Church there is an inscription in Latin commemorating this event: *'Pendentis, Pendente Dei verba accepit aure accipit et verbum corde Brigitta Deum. Anno Jubilei MCCCL"* "He *who is attentive, receives with care in his heart the word and riches of Bridget of God. Jubilee Year 1350.'*

For a long time Saint Bridget wished to know the number of scourges that Our Lord received in His Passion. One day, Jesus Christ appeared to her, saying:

'I received 5480 blows on My Body. If you wish to honor them in some way, say 15 Our Fathers and 15 Hail Mary's with the following Prayers (which He taught her) for a whole year. When the year is up, you will have honored each one of My Wounds.'

Then Our Lord made the following **Promises** to the persons who dedicate themselves to recite these prayers for a whole year.

The 15 Magnificent Promises

I will deliver 15 souls of his lineage from Purgatory.

15 souls of his lineage will be confirmed and preserved in grace.

15 sinners of his lineage will be converted.

Whoever recites these Prayers will attain in the first degree of perfection.

15 days before his death I will give him My Precious Body in order that he may escape eternal starvation; I will give him My Precious Blood to drink lest he thirst eternally.

15 days before his death he will feel a deep contrition for all his sins and will have a perfect knowledge of them.

I will place before him the sign of My Victorious Cross for his help and defense against the attacks of his enemies.

Before his death I shall come with My Dearest Beloved Mother.

I shall graciously receive his soul, and will lead it into eternal joys.

And having led it there I shall give him a special draught from the fountain of My Deity, something I will not for those who have not recited My Prayers.

Let it be known that whoever may have been living in the state of mortal sin for 30 years, but who will recite devoutly, or have the intention to recite these Prayers, the Lord will forgive him all his sins.

I shall protect him from strong temptations.

I shall preserve and guard his 5 senses.

I shall preserve him from a sudden death.

His soul will be delivered from eternal death.

He will obtain all he asks for from God and the Blessed Virgin

If he has lived all his life doing his own will and he is to die the next day, his life will be prolonged.

Every time one recites these Prayers he gains 100 days indulgence.

He is assured of being joined to the supreme Choir of Angels.

Whoever teaches these Prayers to another, will have continuous joy and merit which will endure eternally.

There where these prayer are being said or will be said in the future God is present with His grace.

The Fifteen Prayers

First Prayer
Our Father – Hail Mary. O Jesus Christ! Eternal Sweetness to those who love Thee, joy surpassing all joy and all desire, Salvation and Hope of all sinners. Who hast proved that Thou hast no greater desire than to be among men, even assuming human nature at the fullness of time for the love of men, recall all the sufferings Thou hast endured from the instant of Thy conception, and especially during Thy Passion, as it was decreed and ordained from all eternity in the Divine plan.

Remember, O Lord, that during the Last Super with Thy disciples, having washed their feet, Thou gavest them Thy Most Precious Body and Blood, and while at the same time Thou didst sweetly console them, Thou didst foretell them Thy coming Passion.

Remember the sadness and bitterness which Thou didst experience in Thy Soul as Thou Thyself bore witness saying: "My Soul is sorrowful even unto death."

Remember all the fear, anguish and pain that Thou didst suffer in Thy delicate Body before the torment of the Crucifixion, when, after having prayed three times, bathed in a sweat of blood, Thou wast betrayed by Judas, Thy disciple, arrested by the people of a nation Thou hadst chosen and elevated, accused by false witnesses, unjustly judged by three judges during the flower of Thy youth and during the solemn Paschal season. Remember that Thou wast despoiled of Thy garments and clothed in those of derision; that Thy Face and Eyes were veiled, that Thou wast buffeted, crowned with thorns, a reed placed in Thy Hands, that Thou was crushed with blows and overwhelmed with affronts and outrages. In memory of all these pains and sufferings which Thou didst endure before Thy Passion on the Cross, grant me before my death true contrition, a sincere and entire confession, worthy satisfaction and the remission of all my sins. Amen

Second Prayer

Our Father – Hail Mary. O Jesus! True liberty of angels, Paradise of delights, remember the horror and sadness which Thou didst endure when Thy enemies, like furious lions, surrounded Thee, and by thousands of insults, spits, blows, lacerations and other unheard-of-cruelties, tormented Thee at will. Through these torments and insulting words, I beg Thee, O my Savior, to deliver me from all my enemies, visible and invisible, and under Thy protection, may I attain the perfection of eternal salvation. Amen.

Third Prayer

Our Father – Hail Mary. O Jesus! Creator of Heaven and earth Whom nothing can encompass or limit. Thou Who dost enfold and hold all under Thy Loving power. Remember the very bitter pain Thou didst suffer when the Jews nailed Thy Sacred Hands and Feet to the Cross by blow after blow with big blunt nails, and not finding Thee in a pitiable enough state to satisfy their rage, they enlarged Thy Wounds, and added pain to pain, and with indescribable cruelty stretched Thy Body on the Cross, pulled Thee from all sides, thus dislocating Thy Limbs. I beg of Thee, O Jesus, by the memory of this most Loving suffering of the Cross, to grant me the grace to fear Thee and to Love Thee. Amen.

Fourth Prayer
Our Father – Hail Mary. O Jesus! Heavenly Physician, raised aloft on the Cross in order that through Thy wounds ours might be healed, remember the bruises which Thou didst suffer and the weakness of all Thy Members which were distended to such a degree that never was there pain like unto Thine. From the crown of Thy Head to the Soles of Thy Feet there was not one spot on Thy Body that was not in torment, and yet, forgetting all Thy sufferings, Thou didst not cease to pray to Thy heavenly Father for Thy enemies, saying "Father forgive them for they know not what they do."

Through this great Mercy, and in memory of this suffering, grant that the remembrance of Thy Most Bitter Passion may effect in us a perfect contrition and the remission of all our sins. Amen.

Fifth Prayer
Our Father – Hail Mary. O Jesus! Mirror of eternal splendor, remember the sadness which Thou experienced, when contemplating in the light of Thy Divinity the predestination of those who would be saved by the merits of Thy Sacred passion, Thou didst see at the same time, the great multitude of reprobates who would be damned for their sins, and Thou didst complain bitterly of those hopeless lost and unfortunate sinners.
Through this abyss of compassion and pity, and especially through the goodness which Thou displayed to the good thief when Thou saidst to him: "This day, thou shalt be with Me in paradise." I beg of Thee, O Sweet Jesus, that at the hour of my death, Thou wilt show me mercy. Amen.

Sixth Prayer
Our Father – Hail Mary. O Jesus! Beloved and most desirable King, remember the grief Thou didst suffer, when naked and like a common criminal, Thou was fastened and raised on the Cross, when all Thy relatives and friends abandoned Thee, except Thy Beloved Mother, who remained close to Thee during Thy agony and whom Thou didst entrust to Thy faithful disciple when Thou saidst to Mary: "Woman, behold thy son!" and to Saint John: "Son, behold thy Mother!"

I beg of Thee O my Savior, by the sword of sorrow which pierced the soul of Thy holy Mother, to have compassion on me in all my affliction and tribulations, both corporal and spiritual, and to assist me in all my trials, and especially at the hour of my death. Amen.

Seventh Prayer
Our Father – Hail Mary. O Jesus! Inexhaustible Fountain of compassion, Who by a profound gesture of Love, said from the Cross: "I thirst!" suffered from the thirst for the salvation of the human race. I beg of Thee O my Savior, to inflame in our hearts the desire to tend toward perfection in all our acts; and to extinguish in us the concupiscence of the flesh and the ardor of worldly desires. Amen.

Eighth Prayer
Our Father – Hail Mary. O Jesus! Sweetness of hearts, delight of the spirit, by the bitterness of the vinegar and gall which Thou didst taste on the Cross for Love of us, grant us the grace to receive worthily Thy Precious Body and Blood during our life and at the hour of our death, that they may serve as a remedy and consolation for our souls. Amen

Ninth Prayer
Our Father – Hail Mary. O Jesus! Royal virtue, joy of the mind, recall the pain Thou didst endure when, plunged in an ocean of bitterness at the approach of death; insulted, outraged by the Jews, Thou didst cry out in a loud voice that Thou was abandoned by Thy Father, saying: "My God, My God, why hast Thou forsaken me?"

Through this anguish, I beg of Thee, O my Savior, not to abandon me in the terrors and pains of my death. Amen

Tenth Prayer
Our Father – Hail Mary. O Jesus! Who art the beginning and end of all things, life and virtue, remember that for our sakes Thou wast plunged in an abyss of suffering from the Soles of Thy Feet to the crown of Thy Head. In consideration of the enormity of Thy Wounds, teach me to keep, through pure love, Thy Commandments, whose way is wide and easy for those who love Thee. Amen

Eleventh Prayer
Our Father – Hail Mary. O Jesus! Deep abyss of mercy, I beg of Thee, in memory of Thy Wounds which penetrated to the very marrow of Thy Bones and to the depth of Thy being, to draw me, a miserable sinner, overwhelmed by my offenses, away from sin and to hide me from Thy Face justly irritated against me, hide me in Thy Wounds, until Thy anger and just indignation shall have passed away. Amen

Twelfth Prayer
Our Father – Hail Mary. O Jesus! Mirror of Truth, symbol of unity, link of Charity, remember the multitude of wounds with

which Thou wast afflicted from head to foot, torn and reddened by the spilling of Thy adorable blood. O great and universal pain which Thou didst suffer in Thy virginal Flesh for Love of us! Sweetest Jesus! What is there that Thou couldst have done for us which Thou hast not done? May the fruit of Thy sufferings be renewed in my soul by the faithful remembrance of Thy passion, and may Thy Love increase in my heart each day, until I see Thee in eternity, Thou Who art the treasury of every real good and every joy, which I beg Thee to grant me, O sweetest Jesus, in Heaven. Amen

Thirteenth Prayer
Our Father – Hail Mary. O Jesus! Strong Lion, Immortal and Invincible King, remember the pain which Thou didst endure when all Thy strength, both moral and physical, was entirely exhausted, Thou didst bow Thy head, saying: "All is consummated!". Through this anguish and grief, I beg of Thee Lord Jesus, to have mercy on me at the hour of my death, when my mind will be greatly troubled and my soul will be in anguish. Amen

Fourteenth Prayer
Our Father – Hail Mary. O Jesus! Only Son of the Father, splendor and figure of His substance remember the simple and humble recommendation Thou didst make of Thy Soul to Thy Eternal Father, saying: "Father, into Thy Hands I commend My Spirit!", and when Thy body, all torn, and Thy Heart broken, and the bowels of Thy Mercy open to redeem us, Thou didst Expire. By this Precious Death, I beg of Thee O King of Saints, comfort me and help me to resist the devil, the flesh and the world, so that being dead to the world, I may

live for Thee alone. I beg of Thee at the hour of my death to receive me, a pilgrim and an exile returning to Thee. Amen

Fifteenth Prayer
Our Father – Hail Mary. O Jesus! True and fruitful Vine! Remember the abundant outpouring of Blood which Thou didst so generously shed from Thy Sacred Body pressed down and running over as the grape crushed in the wine press.

From Thy Side, pierced with a lance by a soldier, blood and water issued forth until there was not left in Thy Body a single drop, and finally, like a bundle of myrrh lifted to the very top of the Cross, Thy delicate flesh was destroyed, the very Substance of Thy Body withered, and the Marrow of Thy Bones dried up.

Through this bitter Passion and through the outpouring of Thy precious Blood, I beg of Thee, O Sweet Jesus, to pierce my heart so that my tears of penitence and love will be my bread day and night. May I be converted entirely to Thee, may my heart be Thy perpetual resting place, may my conversation be pleasing to Thee, and my the end of my life be so praiseworthy that I may merit Heaven and there with Thy saints, praise Thee forever. Amen

The 17 Promises of Our Lord to Those Who Practice the Devotion of the Rosary of the Holy Wounds

This Rosary to the Holy Wounds and the 17 promises were revealed by Our Lord to Sister Mary Martha Chambon (1842-1907), of the Monastery of the Visitation of Chambery.

At each word that you pronounce of the Chaplet of the Holy Wounds, I allow a drop of My Blood to fall upon the soul of a sinner.

Each time that you offer to My Father the merits of My Divine Wounds, you win an immense fortune.

Souls that will have contemplated and honored My crown of thorns on earth, will be My crown of glory in Heaven!

I will grant all that is asked of Me through the invocation of My Holy Wounds. You will obtain everything, because it is through the merit of My Blood, which is of infinite price. With My Wounds and My Divine Heart, everything can be obtained.

From My Wounds proceed fruits of sanctity. As gold purified in the crucible becomes more beautiful, so you must put your soul and those of your companions into My sacred Wounds; there they will become perfected as gold in the furnace. You can always purify yourself in My Wounds.

My Wounds will repair yours. My Wounds will cover all your faults. Those who honor them will have a true knowledge of Jesus Christ. In meditation on them, you will always find a new love. My Wounds will cover all your sins.

Plunge your actions into My Wounds and they will be of value. All your actions, even the least, soaked in My Blood, will acquire by this alone an infinite merit and will please My Heart.

In offering My Wounds for the conversion of sinners, even though the sinners are not converted, you will have the same merit before God as if they were.

When you have some trouble, something to suffer, quickly place it in My Wounds, and the pain will be alleviated.

This aspiration must often be repeated near the sick: "My Jesus, pardon and mercy through the merits of Thy Holy Wounds!" This prayer will solace soul and body.

A sinner who will say the following prayer will obtain conversion: "Eternal Father, I offer Thee the Wounds of our Lord Jesus Christ to heal those of our souls."

There will be no death for the soul that expires in My Holy Wounds; they give true life.

This chaplet is a counterpoise to My justice; it restrains My vengeance.

Those who pray with humility and who meditate on My Passion, will one day participate in the glory of My Divine Wounds.

The more you will have contemplated My painful Wounds on this earth, the higher will be your contemplation of them glorious in Heaven.

The soul who during life has honored the Wounds of our Lord Jesus Christ and has offered them to the Eternal Father for the Souls in Purgatory, will be accompanied at the moment of death by the Holy Virgin and the Angels; and Our Lord on the Cross, all brilliant in glory, will receive her and crown her.

The invocations of the Holy Wounds will obtain an incessant victory for the Church.

'I will grant all that you request by the invocation of My Holy Wounds.'

Jesus asked that we say the devotion to His Holy Wounds 'You will obtain everything because it is the merit of my Blood, which is of infinite price [...] With my Wounds and my Divine Heart, you can obtain everything.'

'My Wounds will save you infallibly [...] They will save the world. There will be no death for the soul that expires in my Wounds; they give true life.'

In favor of the sick

'Close to the sick one must often repeat this aspiration: 'My Jesus, pardon and mercy by the merits of your Holy Wounds!' This prayer will relieve the soul and the body.'

In favor of the sinner

'When you offer my Wounds for sinners, you must not forget to do so for the souls in Purgatory, because few people think of relieving them.'

In favor of the souls in Purgatory

'When you offer My Holy Wounds for sinners, you must not forget to do so for the souls in Purgatory, as there are but few who think of their relief. The Holy Wounds are the treasure of treasures for the souls in Purgatory.'

Rosary of the Holy Wounds

Pray the following prayers on the crucifix and on the first 3 beads:

V. O Jesus, Divine Redeemer, Have Mercy on us and on the whole world.

R. Amen.

V. Holy God, Holy Mighty One, Holy Immortal One.

R. Have Mercy on us and on the whole world.

V. Grace and Mercy, O my Jesus, during present dangers; cover us with Your Most Precious Blood.

R. Amen.

V. Eternal Father, show us your Mercy through the Blood of your beloved Son. We beg you, show us your Mercy.

R. Amen.

After each Wound pray with devotion:

In the large beads (those of the Our Father), say once:

V. Eternal Father, I offer You the Wounds of our Lord Jesus Christ.

R. To heal the wounds of our souls.

In the small beads (those of the Hail Mary) say ten times:

V. My Jesus, piety and Mercy.

R. By the merits of your Holy Wounds.

The Wounds of the Feet

Crucified Lord, I adore the Sacred Wounds of Your Feet, by the pain that You endured and the blood that You shed, grant me the grace to avoid sin and to follow constantly, until the end of my life, the path of Christian virtues.

Eternal Father...

Wound of the Sacred Side

Crucified Lord, I adore the Wound of Your Sacred Side, by the blood that You shed, I beg You to enkindle in my heart the fire of Divine Love and to grant me the grace to love You eternally

Eternal Father...

Wound of the Left Hand

Crucified Lord, I adore the Sacred Wound of Your Left Hand, by the pain that You endured and the blood that You shed, I beg You not to let me be found on Your left side with the condemned the day of the Final Judgment.

Eternal Father...

Wound of the Right Hand

Crucified Lord, I adore the Sacred Wound of Your Right Hand, by the pain that You endured and the blood that You shed, I beg You to bless me and to conduct me to eternal life.

Eternal Father...

Wound of the Head

Crucified Lord, I adore the Sacred Wounds of Your Head, by the pain that You endured and the blood that You shed, I beg You to grant me the grace to serve You and to serve others.

Eternal Father...

At the end of the Rosary, say three times:

V. Eternal Father I offer You the Wounds of Our Lord Jesus Christ

R. To heal the wounds of our souls

Prayer of the Holy Angels for the Souls in Purgatory

Jesus, Our Lord, You spent the night of Your suffering on the Mount of Olives and You saw in the sins of the whole world such a heavy burden that You sweated blood. The disciples were asleep and Your Heavenly Father sent an Angel to console and strengthen You in your agony.

Look, Lord, at our brothers and sisters in Purgatory. They suffer more than a man could suffer in this world, and You want us to help them.

You have given us the opportunity to help them by watching, praying and offering a sacrifice for them, especially the Holy sacrifice of the Mass. We also send them our Guardian Angels to console and strengthen them with the strength of Your Blood. As God was merciful with You on the *Mount of Olives*, He wants us also to be merciful with the souls of the suffering Church.

Jesus, remember your abandonment on the Mount of Olives and just as the Angel strengthened You, grant the souls the same consolation you received there.

Mary, Queen of Angels, have mercy on Your suffering children in Purgatory. Send Your Angels to help them.

Saint Michael Archangel, Saint Gabriel Archangel, Saint Raphael Archangel, Your Nine Choirs of Angels, Seraphim and Cherubim, Thrones and Dominions, Principalities and Powers, Virtues, Archangels and Angels, in the name of God and in the name of Your Queen, our Heavenly Mother Mary, we ask You to help our brothers in Purgatory. They suffer great punishment and aspire to the Eternal God. Strengthen them and lead them on the path to the Heavenly Homeland. Amen.

Chaplet in Honor of Saint Michael Archangel

Saint Michael Archangel appeared to Antonia d'Astonac, a most devout Servant of God and told her that he wished to be honored by nine salutations, corresponding to the nine Choirs of Angels, which should consist of one Our Father and three Hail Marys in honor of each of the Angelic Choirs.

Promises of Saint Michael

'Whoever would practice this devotion in his honor would have, when approaching the Holy Table (Holy Communion), an escort of nine angels chosen from each of the Choirs. In addition, for the daily recital of these nine salutations, he promised his continual assistance and that of all the holy angels during life, and after death deliverance from Purgatory for themselves and all their relations.'

Chaplet

Act of contrition and supplication.

My God, I repent for having offended you because you are infinitely good and kind; through your holy grace, I firmly propose not to offend you again, even at the cost of my life.

Lord, by your infinite power and virtue, and by the merits of the Passion and Death of your glorious Son, I beg you for a clean heart, a controlled tongue, and to offer good works to please you. Amen.

Say over Saint Michael's medal:

V. My God, come to my aid!

R. Lord, make haste to help me.

Glory be to the Father, and to the Son, and to the Holy Spirit as it was in the beginning is now, and ever shall be, world without end. Amen

First Salutation
My God! By the intercession of Saint Michael Archangel and the Heavenly Choir of the Seraphim, enkindle in our hearts the flame of perfect charity.

Saint Michael Archangel, defend us in the battle, may we not perish in the tremendous judgment of God (This last invocation is repeated at the end of each Salutation).

One Our Father and three Hail Marys.

Second Salutation
My God! Through the intercession of Saint Michael Archangel and the Heavenly Choir of the Cherubim, grant us the grace to leave the path of sin and follow that of Christian perfection.

Saint Michael Archangel, defend us .... One Our Father & three Hail Marys.

Third Salutation
My God! Through the intercession of Saint Michael Archangel and of the Heavenly Choir of the Thrones, infuse in our hearts a spirit of true and sincere humility.

Saint Michael Archangel, defend us ... One Our Father and three Hail Marys.

Fourth Salutation
My God! Through the intercession of Saint Michael Archangel and of the Heavenly Choir of the Dominions, grant us the grace to control our senses and correct our passions.

Saint Michael Archangel, defend us ... One Our Father and three Hail Marys.

Fifth Salutation
My God! Through the intercession of Saint Michael Archangel and the Heavenly Choir of the Powers, deign to protect our souls against the snares and temptations of the devil.

Saint Michael Archangel, defend us ... One Our Father and three Hail Marys.

Sixth Salutation
My God! Through the intercession of Saint Michael Archangel and of the Heavenly Choir of the Virtues, do not let us fall into temptation, but deliver us from evil.

Saint Michael Archangel, defend us ... One Our Father and three Hail Marys.

Seventh Salutation

My God! Through the intercession of Saint Michael Archangel and of the Heavenly Choir of the Principalities, fill our souls with the spirit of true and sincere obedience.

Saint Michael Archangel, defend us … One Our Father and three Hail Marys.

Eighth Salutation

My God! Through the intercession of Saint Michael Archangel and of the Heavenly Choir of the Archangels, grant us perseverance in faith, hope, charity, piety, prayer and good works, to be able to possess eternal glory.

Saint Michael Archangel, defend us … One Our Father and three Hail Marys.

Ninth Salutation

My God! Through the intercession of Saint Michael Archangel and of the Heavenly Choir of the Angels, deign to grant us the protection in this mortal life and then take us to the glory of Heaven. Amen.

Saint Michael Archangel, defend us …One Our Father and three Hail Marys.

Then pray four Our Fathers, the first in honor of Saint Michael, the second in honor of Saint Gabriel, the third in honor of Saint Raphael and the fourth in honor of our Guardian Angel.

Invocation
O glorious Prince Saint Michael, Leader and Commander of the Heavenly Host, Guardian of souls, Vanquisher of rebel spirits, Servant in the house of the Divine King, and our glorious Guide, thou art brilliant in holiness and power.

Deliver us from all evil, for we turn to thee with confidence and enable us by thy gracious protection to serve God more faithfully everyday.

V. Pray for us, O most glorious protector, Saint Michael, Prince of the Church of Jesus Christ!

R. That we may be worthy to obtain his promises.

Prayer
Almighty and everlasting God, since in Your infinite goodness and mercy You desire the salvation of all men, You hast appointed the most glorious Archangel, Saint Michael Prince of Your Church. Make us worthy, we beg of Thee to be delivered by his powerful protection from all our enemies, that we may not be overcome by them at the hour of death, but that we may be conducted by Saint Michael into the holy presence of Thy Divine Majesty. This, we beg through the merits of Jesus Christ Our Lord. Amen.

INDULGENCES

In addition to all that has been mentioned in this book and in the previous chapter about the great help we can give the holy souls in through the devotions, we must also consider the great benefit that the Church has granted us through indulgences.

An indulgence is a remission of the temporal pain, namely the punishment (Purgatory) which we deserve for having offended God.

When a mortal sin is committed, the soul is mortally wounded; that wound kills the soul, all grace is lost and if the person does not repent, he is damned. If he is able to confess his sin, his wound is healed and will not be condemned. But a scar remains. Even those sins that are forgiven leave scars which are purified in Purgatory. Historically, plenary indulgences were first granted in the Eleventh Century to all those who visited the church of Our Lady of the Angels called The Porciuncula. The Lord granted it on the condition that it was approved by the Pope, which Honorius III granted in 1221.

Later, the jubilee plenary indulgence was introduced, beginning in 1300 (Boniface VII) The jubilee that was reduced to fifty years, to thirty and finally to twenty-five in 1470 (Paul II).

At the beginning in the Fourteenth Century, the concession of indulgences was multiplied and later on, in the Fifteenth Century, the indulgences for the dead were extended.

Indulgences can be plenary or partial. *Plenary indulgences* can be gained on special days assigned by the Church, in which a number of conditions are exacted to obtain their benefit.

Among the most important conditions we can point out, is the need to understand the seriousness of this commitment to God. In order to obtain such an immeasurable blessing, the soul must be completely immersed in a sincere act of contrition during reconciliation and it must have the awareness that every 'mortal' sin confessed was of a grave nature. Mortal sin can kill the soul eternally; it offends God enormously, and harms the Church and impacts one's neighbor. If we knew the extent of this, we would prefer to die rather than to sin again.

If we achieve this dimension of reconciliation and awareness, we will obtain immense blessings. Sincerity and contrition are imperative to be fully reconciled. Reconciliation cannot be received by merely completing this religious action through obligation or mechanically.

This indulgence promises to free us completely from our pending temporal punishment, which means that if we died after receiving it, we would go straight to Heaven.

If, instead, we gave up the benefits and indulgences we receive and offered them up for a soul or for souls in Purgatory, after having done what is indicated above, it would have much more merit. In God's Mercy, a soul in Purgatory will be chosen by God, to receive such benefits so that it can be taken to Heaven.

Requirements to gain a plenary indulgence:

Confession.
Communion
Prayers for the intentions of the Holy Father.
Our Father, Hail Mary, Glory be and Creed.
No attachment to any sin whatsoever.

If one of these conditions is lacking, only a partial indulgence is gained. A plenary indulgence is gained only on the day, except in the case of death.

Confession can be made a few days before or after doing the work (understanding by work what we will subsequently enumerate).

Communion and prayer for the Pope can also be done a few days after or before the work, but it is recommended to do it the same day. There must be no attachment for any sin whatsoever. For God to forgive us completely of a sin, even if it is venial, we must be totally repentant and make the firm decision not to commit the sin again.

It is an excellent devotion – much loved by the Saints and recommended by them and by great theologians –, to try to gain a plenary indulgence every day.

A plenary indulgence is gained by:

Praying the Holy Rosary: an unbroken recitation and meditation of the five mysteries, to be said in a church or oratory. In the family, in Religious Communities or pious Associations (such as the Cenacles of prayer or prayer groups).

The Holy *Via Crucis,* prayed before erected Stations. It is sufficient to mediate on the Passion and Death of the Lord. The consideration of each Station is not necessary (each Station can be read attentively). The fourteen Stations must be made (if many do them publicly, it is sufficient if the one leading them covers them).

Adoration of the Most Holy Sacrament for the space of half an hour.

Reading the Bible for half an hour a day.

Visit to the Patriarchal Basilicas of Rome.

A blessing from the Holy Father for the whole World, even if it is by radio.

Visit to a cemetery from the 1st to the 8th of November.

Adoration of the Cross on Good Friday.

The prayer 'Behold me prostrated here' before a Crucifix after Communion, on the Fridays of Lent and of Passion week.

Attendance at the Solemn Closing of a Eucharistic Congress.

Spiritual Exercises, at least for three days.

Act of Reparation in public on the day of the Sacred Heart of Jesus.

Apostolic Blessing *"in articulo mortis."*

Mission, attendance at some of the preaching and the closing.

First Communion for the one making it and those attending.

A priest's first Mass and those attending, if the Mass is celebrated with some solemnity.

Priestly Jubilee: twenty-five, fifty and sixty years.

Visit to the Station Churches of Rome.

Solemn *"Tantum Ergo"* on Maundy Thursday and the day of *Corpus Christi.*

Public *"Te Deum"* on the last day of the year.

Public *"Veni Creator"* on New Year's Day and Pentecost.

Visit to the Titular's Parish Church and on August 2 (The Porciuncula).

Visit to a Church or Oratory on All Souls Day.

Visit a Church during a pastoral visit.

Visit a Church or Oratory of a Religious Order on the day of their Holy Founder.

Renewal of the Baptismal promises at the Easter Vigil and on the anniversary of Baptism, using any formula.

A *partial indulgence* is forgiveness of part of the punishment. It is gained by being in a state of grace and by having the intention to receive it.

A partial indulgence is gained as follows:

A partial indulgence is granted to the Christian faithful who, in fulfilling their duties and in the suffering of life's miseries, raise their souls to God with humble trust, even if only mentally, with a pious invocation. In other words, virtually all prayers, including short prayers, are indulgenced. The exception is if they are prayed without humility and trust.

A partial indulgence is granted to the Christian faithful who, bearing the spirit of faith, offer themselves or their goods in the service of their needy brothers with a spirit of mercy. An indulgence is granted for any work of charity done in a Christian spirit (not out of vanity). It will be greater, the greater the offering, for instance, alms, the sacrifice it entails and the love with which it is done, etc.

A partial indulgence is granted to the faithful who voluntarily abstain from licit and pleasurable things, out of a spirit of penance.

In addition to the three previous general concessions, a partial; indulgence is granted to

All prayers that the Church recommends especially, for instance: the Rosary, the Creed, Spiritual Communion, Act of Contrition, etc.

The pious use of: crucifixes, crosses, Rosaries, scapulars, medals, among others, which are blessed by a priest.

Bishops can grant certain indulgences to their subjects and to all in their Diocese.

The Constitution on Indulgences *Indulgentiarum Doctrina,* promulgated by Paul VI on January 1, 1967, states: 'still today the Church invites all her children to consider and ponder how good it is to use indulgences to foster each one's Christian life, more than that, that of the whole society [...], she recommends again to all her faithful the use of Indulgences, very pleasing to the Christian people for many centuries and also in our time.' (Taken from *Indulgences,* Treasures of the Church. Juan Gutierrez Ortiz, Published by the Jesus of Mercy Foundation).

BIBLIOGRAPHY

- Catechism of the Catholic Church. *Sure norm for the teaching of the faith.* John Paul II.
- Councils of the Catholic Church.
- *Navarre Bible.* Popular Edition. EUNSA.
- General Audiences of the Holy Fathers, Blessed John Paul II, His Holiness Benedict XVI (www.vatican.va).
- Encyclical *Spe Salvi.*
- Web page (www.apologeticasiloe.com).
- *Catacombs of Rome and Catholic Doctrine,* Dom Maurus Wolter, Tequi Publishers, Paris, 1872. Translated from the French by Dr. Julio Lopez Morales.
- *Purgatory, the Primitive Church, the Fathers of the Church.* By Jose Maria Arraiz. The Internet.
- *Purgatory Quizzes to a Street Preacher.* (Page 2). Written by Father Charles M. Carty & Reverend Dr. Rumble, M.S.C. Tan Books and Publishers, Inc., 1976.
- *Purgatory: The Last of God's Mercies.* Father Dolindo Ruotolo. (Foyer N.S. del Carmen - Casilla 15 - Tome, Chile).
- *A Visit of Purgatory,* produced by the Digital Review *Fides et Ratio.*
- *Manuscript on Purgatory.* Libreria Espiritual. Av. Eloy Alfaro No. 466 and 9th of October, PO BOX 6252 - CCI - Quito.
- *La Pieta Prayer book.* Published in the United States by M1or Corporation.
- Homilies of the Holy Cure of Ars
- *Great Promises of the Virgin.* Jeremias Lopez. Page 150, Libreria Espiritual ("Future of Spain in the Fatima Documents." By Antonio Maria Martins, SJ, page 132, Ediciones Catolicas Publishers, Maldonado, 1.280006, Madrid).

- *Read Me or Rue It*: EDM, Engant de Marie. Father O. Sullivan. Page www.scribd.com/doc48541181 Libro-Almas -del-Purgatorio.
- *The Poor Souls*. A Padre Pio Reminder. By Reverend Paul O'Sullivan, O.P. [Original title: *Read Me or Rue It*] National Center for Padre Pio, Inc.
- *The Holy Souls*. Friar Alessio Parente OFM Cap. Padre Pio da Pietrelcina Editions. Third Edition, 2004.
- *Voce di Padre Pio*, Bulletin II, No. 5 (1978): 15.
- Iasanzaniro M. (Father), ms 1-2).
- Diary. *Divine Mercy in My Soul*. Saint Maria Faustina Kowalska. Published by the Marian Fathers of the Immaculate Conception of the Most Holy Virgin Mary. Stockbridge, Massachusetts, 1987.
- *Complete Visions and Revelations*. Anne Catherine Emmerick. According to Annotations of Clement Brentano. First Tome, Book 3. Autobiography and General Visions, Mexico D.F.
- *Purgatory*, by Father F.X. Schouppe, S.J. Translated from the French. Tan Books and Publishers, Inc., 1998.
- *Para Salvarte*. Jorge Loring, S.J., 45th edition. Editorial Testimonio. Madrid.
- *Prayer book to the Holy Angels, a Compilation of Prayers to the Angels Taken from the Tradition of the Church*, by Father Cornelio Pfeifer ORC. Sixth Edition, Order of Canons Regular of the Holy Cross.
- *The Holy Wounds of Our Lord Jesus Christ*. Sister Maria Martha Chambon. Fifth Edition, Convent of the Visitation.
- *Knock: Vision of Hope*. Father Hubert, O.F.M. Cap. Published by the Knock Shrine Society.
- *The Soul Enamored of the Child Jesus,* Volume 2, July-December. Blessed Lorenzo Maria de San Francisco Saverio, Passionist priest, missionary of the Divine Child

Jesus. Original title: *L'Anima Innamorata di Gesu Bambino.* From whom he receives every day. Brief Spiritual Invitations. Sixth Edition. Rome, 1870.

- *The Glories of Mary.* Saint Alphonsus Mary Liguori, Bishop, Doctor and Founder of the Congregation of the Most Holy Redeemer. Translated by J.J. Itoiz y Leoz, C.SS.R., Editorial Cobarrubias 19, 28010 Madrid.
- *Indulgences: The Treasures of the Church.* Juan Gutierrez Ortiz. Jesus of Mercy Foundation Edition. Libreria Espiritual.